# Facing Age

# Diversity and Aging

*Series Editor*
**Toni Calasanti**
*Virginia Tech*

The elder population is not only growing in size, but also becoming more diverse—including differences in gender, race, ethnicity, class, and sexuality—and the experiences of aging people can vary dramatically. Books in this series explore this diversity, focusing on the ways that these social inequalities, along with ageism, shape experiences of growing old. The series will illustrate the challenges and opportunities that diversity and aging present for society, both now and in the future.

*Facing Age: Women Growing Older in Anti-Aging Culture*
    Laura Hurd Clarke

# Facing Age

## Women Growing Older in Anti-Aging Culture

Laura Hurd Clarke

ROWMAN & LITTLEFIELD PUBLISHERS, INC.
*Lanham • Boulder • New York • Toronto • Plymouth, UK*

Published by Rowman & Littlefield Publishers, Inc.
A wholly owned subsidiary of The Rowman & Littlefield Publishing Group, Inc.
4501 Forbes Boulevard, Suite 200, Lanham, Maryland 20706
http://www.rowmanlittlefield.com

Estover Road, Plymouth PL6 7PY, United Kingdom

British Library Cataloguing in Publication Information Available

**Library of Congress Cataloging-in-Publication Data**

Clarke, Laura Hurd, 1969–
  Facing age : women growing older in anti-aging culture / Laura Hurd Clarke.
      p. cm. — (Diversity and aging)
  Includes bibliographical references and index.
  ISBN 978-1-4422-0759-2 (cloth : alk. paper) — ISBN 978-1-4422-0760-8 (pbk. :
alk. paper) — ISBN 978-1-4422-0761-5 (electronic)
  1. Beauty, Personal. 2. Middle-aged women—Psychology. 3. Aging—
Psychological aspects. 4. Middle-aged women—Physiological aspects. 5.
Feminine beauty (Aesthetics) 6. Self-esteem in women. I. Title.
  HQ1219.C53 2011
  306.4'613—dc22                                                            2010023866

Printed in the United States of America

To Ayden and Alyssa, with all my love.

# Contents

# Acknowledgments

This book would not have happened if Toni Calasanti had not afforded me the opportunity, encouragement, and mentorship required to bring it to fruition. I am truly grateful and have learned more than I could have imagined through this process. Thank you.

This book would also not have happened without the undying patience and love of my husband, Darryl, the enthusiastic cheerleading of my dearest friend, Tricia, the sage advice of my colleagues at the University of British Columbia, the assistance of people like Alexandra Korotchenko, Andrea Bundon, and Meridith Griffin, or the inspiration of my parents and grandparents. To all of you, I extend my deepest and most heartfelt appreciation.

Finally, I am entirely indebted to all of the women who have participated in my research and who have given so generously of their time over the past 10 years. Your willingness to share your stories, strength, and pain has changed my life forever.

# 1

⚜

# Introduction

"You are only as old as you look." "You can control how you age."
"Inner beauty is important but not nearly as important as outer
beauty." "Keep them guessing about your age."

Heightening anxiety and ambivalence about the physical realities
of growing older and the concomitant loss of social currency,
these types of statements can be found in advertisements, beauty
columns, talk shows, Internet websites, Hollywood movies, television programs about cosmetic surgery or fashion makeovers, and
motivational posters in fitness gyms. Even the emergence of the Dove
Campaign for Real Beauty, with its co-opting of feminist critiques
and use of alternative and supposedly resistant images of feminine
attractiveness, albeit for the sake of blatantly promoting consumption,
has done little to wrest the hold that restrictive appearance ideals for
women have on Western society (Dye, 2009; Johnston & Taylor, 2008).
Underlying these messages is an increasingly unobtainable beauty
standard for women, which is epitomized by a young, thin, toned,
healthy, White, suntanned body with flawless and wrinkle-free skin,
perfectly coiffed hair, little or no body hair, artfully applied makeup,
and the latest fashionable trappings. Approximation to this beauty
ideal is one of the primary ways by which women are afforded social
value (Bartky, 1998; Bordo, 2003; Brown & Jasper, 1993; Cepanec &

1

Payne, 2000; Dworkin, 1974; Hesse-Biber, 1996; Jeffreys, 2005; Wolf, 1991). Thus, aging poses a huge threat to women's sense of identity, perceived femininity, and sexual desirability. However, Seid (1989) has argued that "[a]ge is an enemy of beauty, but it need not be. If we discipline ourselves . . . we, too, will preserve the source of our beauty, a youthful body" (p. 17). Consequently, Holstein (2006) contends that "ironically, after years of struggle, as women have achieved a stronger status as agents than ever before, we face an escalating set of expectations about our bodies" (p. 320). Indeed, the scope of beauty work, which Kwan and Trautner (2009) define as "specific appearance and beauty practices performed on oneself . . . to elicit certain benefits within a specific social hierarchy" (p. 50), continues to expand with the development of more and more beauty products and services as well as the relentless mining of the female body for potential "flaws" in need of beauty interventions. Reflecting the societal obsession with youthfulness and appearance, ageist media messages depict later life and signs of aging as the products of objectionable, or at the very least indolent, choices that individuals make when they fail to embrace consumerism and the anti-aging movement. Moreover, assumptions about the importance of anti-aging technologies and practices have become unquestioningly entrenched such that there is relatively little critical examination of aging bodies, ageism, and older adults' experiences of oppression within an anti-aging culture.

Despite the ubiquity of anti-aging ideologies and the deep-seated ageist bigotry that underlies contemporary Western society, ageism in all of its manifestations remains undertheorized and underresearched within the sociocultural literature. The disinterest in theorizing and researching age relations partly stems from the privilege of the young who only begin to recognize the power of ageist discourses and discrimination when they themselves become old (Calasanti & Slevin, 2001). In other words, most people choose to ignore or fail to see ageism in society until they are personally touched by the social and physical realities of growing older. Ironically, our disregard of ageism is ultimately to our own detriment since this form of oppression is "the one source of disadvantage that we will all face, should we live long enough" (Calasanti, 2005, p. 8). However, we remain largely unaware of or unwilling to challenge the implications of both our subtle and overt internalization of ageist discourses because conformity to specific norms is required to achieve certain social ends (Holstein, 2006). The taken-for-granted discriminatory discourses and practices surrounding oldness combined with the scholarly silences around aging and aged bodies culminate in our authoring of our own descent into social devaluation. For as Calasanti (2005) aptly states: "We ultimately oppress ourselves: Either we try to avoid the aging process or we lose self-esteem because of the selves we feel we are becoming" (p. 8).

This is not to say that the extant research has completely ignored ageism and the ways that age-based discrimination delimits the lives of older individuals. Sociocultural analyses of ageism have yielded profound insights into the structural inequities that precede and emanate from mandatory retirement policies, negative attitudes toward older workers, lack of access to health care and appropriate caregiving resources, and elder abuse. Seminal works such as those by Arber and Ginn (1991a), Bytheway (1995), Calasanti & Slevin (2001), Cruikshank (2003), Featherstone & Wernick (1995), Furman (1997), Gullette (2004), and Woodward (1999b) have signified influential strides in critical and feminist theorizing about the gendering of later life and the impact and experience of ageism. However, with the exception of Furman's (1997) ethnography of older women and beauty shop culture and the recent scholarship of Brooks (2010) and Kinnunen (2010), the centrality of appearance to age relations[1] and to older women's subjugation as well as the embodied nature of ageism (Laws, 1995) have largely been overlooked. Similar to the disregard of ageism, the reluctance to interrogate the importance of feminine appearance and beauty work practices in women's ongoing experiences of discrimination and oppression stems from the ambivalence with which these aspects of "doing gender" (West & Zimmerman, 1987) are viewed. Furman (1997) contends that women are simultaneously required to engage in beauty work interventions and are held in contempt for doing so, as she asserts the following:

> Our still androcentric culture insists, on the one hand, that women must present attractive appearances if they are to be deemed acceptable and achieve social status. On the other hand, women's preoccupation with appearance is seen as shallow and narcissistic. (p. 3)

Societal ambivalence toward women's bodies, sexuality, and beauty work efforts are further magnified in relation to older women, whose social currency is increasingly jeopardized by their failure to achieve idealized beauty standards and the societal privileging of youth, health, and independence. In this way, the ongoing tendency to ignore older women and older women's bodies within society more broadly, as well as in sociology and feminist theory specifically, combined with the continued privileging of youthfulness mirrors the intense discomfort with which aged femininity, physicality, and sexuality are regarded.

My own journey into the study of aging, beauty work, body image, and embodiment has been an ambivalent one. Witnessing my loved ones age, attending to the voices, appearances, and experiences of aging women, and watching my own body change has often been a difficult task that has forced me to confront my own mortality, humanity, contradictions, and ideological assumptions. The resultant internal struggles intensify daily as I find myself continually reflecting on the impact of sexist and ageist discourses on the futures of my two young children, most especially my daughter. Any investigation into the social and physical realities of growing older is inevitably one that provokes strong and conflicting feelings of anxiety, wonder, incredulity, admiration, despair, hilarity, hope, compassion, revulsion, resilience, denial, rawness, and fear. An examination of embodied female aging is simultaneously political, intensely personal, and fraught with equivocation for the researcher, the researched, and the broader social audience. Just as intersectionality challenged second-wave feminists to rethink their views of patriarchy, so too does the aged female body confront all members of society, should they choose to engage in the confrontation, with the social realities of sexism, ageism, ableism, and other forms of social exclusion and discrimination. Despite the challenges and ambiguities associated with doing this research, I remain hopeful that ageist societal norms regarding later life and the oppressive and often dehumanizing meanings attributed to aging female bodies may be further elucidated, challenged, and transmuted. As society becomes increasingly obsessed with images, appearances, and the pursuit of youthfulness, the aged female body has the potential to become ever more disparaged and ignored even as it gains potential to illuminate, if not explode, societal assumptions and ageist ideals.

## OVERVIEW OF THE BOOK

This book critically examines how women face aging as well as how the face of aging is changing within the context of anti-aging norms and aesthetic medicine. The book draws on 10 years of data collection via five discrete studies, which include three interview studies with older women of varying ages and social locations, one interview study with physicians who provide non-surgical cosmetic procedures, and a content analysis of anti-aging print advertisements found in five women's magazines. Using this multiangled approach, the book provides a nuanced investigation of how women feel about looking and being old, how these feelings and perceptions are framed by cultural norms and medical discourses pertaining to aging, anti-aging, and looking aged, the lengths to which women are willing to go in order to not look old, the ways in which they internalize and resist dominant understandings of beauty and cultural currency, and how these meanings are collectively shaped by the women's various and unique social positions. Smith (1987) has called for a sociology that gives women a voice and thereby "creates the space for an absent subject, and an absent experience that is to be filled with the presence and spoken experience of actual women speaking of and in the actualities of their everyday worlds" (p. 107). To that end, I have relied heavily on the women's narratives with the intention of providing rich and complex insights into how women perceive that cultural discourses are written on and through their aging faces and bodies. The addition of the physician interview data and the content analysis complements the women's narratives and sheds important light on the complexities as well as the insidious nature of anti-aging discourses in contemporary society.

In the chapters that follow, I examine women's embodied and body image experiences of aging and explore women's responses to the physical and social realities of later life using a critical feminist and interpretive lens. As a feminist sociologist, I situate the process and experience of growing older and having an aging and aged female body in a social context that is underscored by sexism and ageism as well as by "the intersection of power relations rooted in gender, racial/ethnic, sexuality, and class hierarchies" (Calasanti & Slevin, 2001, p. 179). Since aging is a relational process in which "the privileged position of one group relies on the disadvantaged position of another" (Calasanti & Slevin, 2001, p. 3), a woman's experience of aging is related to her social location in terms of her age, class, sexual preference, physical ability, and racial/ethnic affiliation, which collectively circumscribe her access to social and economic resources. These points of intersection underscore a woman's internalization of or ability to resist dominant cultural norms concerning later life, physical attractiveness, and gender ideology. Indeed, Laz (2003) states, "we make our own bodies but do not make them just as we please; we do not make them under circumstances chosen by ourselves but under circumstances found, given, and transmitted from the past" (p. 507). In other words, the meanings that a woman attributes to aging, beauty, beauty work, and the physical and social realities of growing older, as well as her ability to effectively and appropriately do gender (West & Zimmerman, 1987) and perform age (Laz, 1998), are shaped by her age, genetic inheritance, and socioeconomic status as well as by her cultural context and historical location.

Chapter 2 reviews the theorizing pertaining to body image, embodiment, and beauty ideology and discusses how these three lenses provide a powerful means of investigating older women's perceptions of and experiences in their aging bodies. To begin, body image refers to how a woman perceives and feels about her body and how much of her sense of feminine identity and self-esteem are invested in her appearance. Since the majority of the existing body image research has been focused on younger and middle-aged women, this book provides an important foray into a largely uncharted territory. At the same time, the concept of embodiment directs attention to what it is like to live in and through an aging female body. While much of the embodied aging research has been concerned with the experience of having various health issues, my use of this theoretical framework analyzes what it is like to be in a body that has wrinkles, sagging skin, gray hair, and other signifiers of advancing age. Finally, an investigation of the influence of beauty ideology contextualizes a woman's body image and embodiment in cultural norms concerning beauty, aging, and the necessities of female appearance work. Beauty and gender norms place a premium on women's looks and establish an impossibly narrow and elusive standard of feminine physical attractiveness that oppresses and excludes older women. Therefore, beauty ideology underscores and reinforces women's tendency to be dissatisfied with their bodies and to experience the process of growing older as one of progressive loss and decay.

Building from the examination of theory, chapter 3 illuminates how older women tend to describe and feel about having and living in their aging bodies. Specifically, I highlight older women's perceptions and experiences of altered body shapes, reflected images, weight, loss of physical function, and health. I use the concepts of body image, embodiment, and beauty ideology to critically examine why older women tend to use words such as "a sagging disaster" and "a maddening disappointment" to describe the physical evolution of their bodies and their feelings about the same.

In chapter 4, I focus on one aspect of the aging body, namely wrinkles, to further investigate women's experiences of facing age. Explicating the impact of anti-aging discourses, I begin by drawing upon interview data with physicians who provide non-surgical cosmetic procedures, such as Botox injections, laser skin treatments, sclerotherapy, hyaluronic acid injections, and microdermabrasion. Physicians maintain that aging must be "fought" against with all available means, including anti-aging beauty work, and that their role is to help women "look good for their ages." In this way, aesthetic physicians embrace and reinforce ageist and sexist norms that depict aged female bodies as unattractive and undesirable, if not unhealthy, and privilege young, slim, wrinkle-free bodies. Next, I compare the findings from one study that was conducted in central Canada before the development of anti-aging aesthetic medicine with the data from a study done in western Canada after products such Botox and Restylane injections began to flood the market. While the women in the first study were equally likely to view their wrinkles as a source of dismay and "badges of honor," the women in the second study had largely internalized the medicalization of wrinkles and had learned to view those facial creases that could be minimized or erased with

Botox, hyaluronic acid, or laser skin treatments as abhorrent and un-necessary. In this way, I demonstrate how women's body image and embodiment have been strongly influenced by pseudoscience and the medicalization of the aging appearance.

In chapter 5, I begin by analyzing print advertisements in five wom-en's magazines and discussing how these are informed by the rise of non-surgical cosmetic procedures and anti-aging discourses. Explor-ing how print advertisements make use of pseudoscientific language to justify and legitimate the product claims, I critically unpack the un-derlying message in these advertisements, namely that to look aged is to be found morally and socially wanting. Next, I examine how older women feel about and interpret media messages regarding beauty and aging. I describe how older women reject the skinny requirement of today's beauty ideal as they refer to contemporary fashion models and Hollywood starlets as "awful," "a damn disgrace," "not normal," and "ugly." I further discuss the tensions that women experience be-tween their internalization of ageist beauty norms and their resistance to media messages that depict the aged female body as unsightly. Thus, I elucidate how the women feel they are influenced by current beauty ideals and the ways in which they internalize and struggle against ageist and sexist cultural norms.

Finally, in chapter 6, I draw on the data and theorizing in the pre-vious chapters to discuss age relations as they pertain to women's body image and embodiment. Bringing together the women's feelings about the physical changes that have occurred and will continue to arise in their bodies, the messages about beauty, aging, and beauty work in the media, and the role of physicians in the beauty business, I situate the many ways that women face aging. In this way, I draw attention to the politics of beauty and the centrality of the body to women's experiences of gendered ageism and the social and physical processes of growing older.

## METHODS AND SAMPLES

This book draws on data from five qualitative research projects that were conducted between 1997 and 2007. The methods and samples of each study are described below.

## Study #1 Older Women's Body Image and Embodied Experience[2]

This study[3] was designed to explore how older, community-dwelling women perceived and made sense of their bodies and the embodied aging process. (See table 1.1.) Conducted in 1999, the study involved 100 hours of in-depth interviewing with 22 women aged 61 to 92 (average age of 77) who were each interviewed at least twice. The participants were residents of a central Canadian city where they were recruited from a local seniors' center (two), two seniors' organizations (four), using advertising on a local community bulletin board television channel (two), and through snowball sampling methods via several contacts in the community (15). While all the women were White and heterosexual, they were diverse in terms of their ages, educational attainments, health statuses, incomes, work histories, and their religious and cultural backgrounds. The women were asked about their life and body histories, their thoughts and feelings about the physical changes that had accompanied aging, and their perceptions of beauty.

## Study #2 Older Women's Perceptions and Experiences of Non-surgical Cosmetic Procedures[4]

This study[5] was focused on older women's perceptions and experiences of non-surgical cosmetic procedures (e.g., Botox injections, chemical peels, injectable fillers, laser hair removal, microdermabrasion, and laser skin treatments). (See table 1.2.) Conducted in 2005, the study involved in-depth interviews with 44 women aged 50 to 70, all of whom, with the exception of two individuals, were interviewed twice for a total of 147 interview hours. While I conducted three-quarters of the interviews, three graduate students, all of whom were female and ranged in age from 25 to 55, conducted the remaining interviews. The women in the nonprobability sample were recruited using advertisements in fitness centers (14), seniors' centers (2), newspapers (19), and snowball sampling methods (9). There was diversity among the women in terms of their age, educational attainment, income, marital status, employment history and status, sexual preference, and country of origin. However, most of the women were aged 50 to 60 (average age of 58) and were heterosexual, relatively well educated, and born in Canada. The women's use of beauty technology was also

**Table 1.1. Study #1**

| Study #1 Sample Characteristics | | *n = 22* |
|---|---|---|
| Age | | |
| | 60–69 | 4 |
| | 70–79 | 9 |
| | 80–89 | 7 |
| | 90–92 | 2 |
| Country of Origin | | |
| | Canada | 15 |
| | Europe | 5 |
| | United States | 2 |
| Education | | |
| | Less Than High School | 3 |
| | High School | 7 |
| | College/University | 11 |
| | Graduate School | 1 |
| Health Issues | | |
| | Arthritis | 13 |
| | Cataracts/Macular Degeneration | 5 |
| | Depression | 3 |
| | Hearing Loss | 7 |
| | Heart Problems | 6 |
| | High Blood Pressure | 5 |
| | High Cholesterol | 4 |
| | History of Breast Cancer | 2 |
| | History of Strokes | 3 |
| | Osteoporosis | 3 |
| | Stress Incontinence | 5 |
| Marital Status | | |
| | Currently Married | 4 |
| | Divorced | 3 |
| | Never Married | 1 |
| | Widowed | 14 |
| Mobility | | |
| | Walks Unassisted | 18 |
| | Use of Cane | 3 |
| | Use of Wheelchair | 1 |
| Residence | | |
| | Apartment | 3 |
| | Condominium | 9 |
| | House | 6 |
| | Retirement Home | 1 |
| | Subsidized Housing | 3 |
| Work History | | |
| | Homemaker | 7 |
| | Worked Part Time | 2 |
| | Worked Full Time | 13 |
| Religious Affiliation | | |
| | Protestant | 14 |
| | Catholic | 2 |
| | Jewish | 2 |
| | Atheist/Unspecified | 4 |

**Table 1.2.   Study #2**

| Study #2 Sample Characteristics | | n = 44 |
|---|---|---|
| Age | | |
| | 50–55 | 16 |
| | 56–60 | 14 |
| | 61–65 | 10 |
| | 66–70 | 4 |
| Education | | |
| | Less Than High School | 1 |
| | High School | 9 |
| | College/University | 22 |
| | Graduate School | 12 |
| Household Income | | |
| | Under $10,000 | 3 |
| | $10–20,000 | 3 |
| | $20–30,000 | 3 |
| | $30–40,000 | 6 |
| | $40–50,000 | 4 |
| | $50–60,000 | 11 |
| | $60–70,000 | 3 |
| | $70,000+ | 9 |
| | Declined to Say | 2 |
| Marital/Partner Status | | |
| | Currently Married/Common-law Partner | 22 |
| | Divorced/Separated | 14 |
| | Widowed | 4 |
| | Never Married | 4 |
| Sexual Preference | | |
| | Heterosexual | 41 |
| | Lesbian | 3 |
| Country of Origin | | |
| | Canada | 37 |
| | Europe | 3 |
| | Asia/South Asia | 2 |
| | Central America | 1 |
| | United States | 1 |
| Beauty Work | | |
| | Anti-wrinkle Creams | 16 |
| | Hair Dyes | 28 |
| | Makeup | 39 |
| | Botox | 6 |
| | Injectable Fillers | 6 |
| | Chemical Peels | 3 |
| | Microdermabrasion | 4 |
| | Photofacials | 4 |
| | Sclerotherapy | 2 |
| | Laser Hair Removal | 3 |
| | Laser Resurfacing | 3 |

(*continued*)

**Table 1.2.   (Continued)**

| Study #2 Sample Characteristics | | n = 44 |
|---|---|---|
| | Acupuncture for Wrinkles | 1 |
| | Liposuction | 1 |
| | Abdominoplasty | 1 |
| | Breast Reduction | 2 |
| | Breast Reconstruction | 1 |
| | Breast Augmentation | 1 |
| Health Issues | | |
| | Anxiety or Depression | 7 |
| | Arthritis | 16 |
| | Breast Reduction | 2 |
| | Cancer | 3 |
| | Fibromyalgia | 4 |
| | Gallbladder Surgery | 5 |
| | Heart Problems | 5 |
| | High Blood Pressure | 7 |
| | High Cholesterol | 5 |
| | Hormone Replacement Therapy | 21 |
| | Thyroid Problems | 4 |
| | Hysterectomy | 8 |
| | Joint Surgery | 2 |
| | Osteopenia or Osteoporosis | 7 |
| | Vision Problems | 15 |

diverse, ranging from those women who had never engaged in any form of beauty work to those who used all available forms of aesthetic intervention, anti-wrinkle creams, hair dyes, makeup, non-surgical procedures, and cosmetic surgery.

## Study #3 The Beauty Work Practices of Women Aged 70+[6]

Conducted in 2007, this study[7] explored the body image and beauty work practices of women aged 70+ and entailed 64 hours of in-depth interviews with 36 women aged 71 to 94. (See table 1.3.) The semi-structured interview schedule consisted of open-ended questions that asked the women to describe their experiences of the use of makeup, hair and nail care, fashion, non-surgical cosmetic procedures, and sunbathing. The women in the nonprobability sample were recruited using advertisements in several local newspapers. Although there was diversity among the women in terms of their age, education,

**Table 1.3. Study #3**

| *Study #3 Sample Characteristics* | | *n = 36* |
|---|---|---|
| Age | | |
| | 70–75 | 14 |
| | 76 80 | 6 |
| | 81 85 | 8 |
| | 86–90 | 7 |
| | 91–95 | 1 |
| Country of Origin | | |
| | Canada | 27 |
| | England | 5 |
| | Scotland | 1 |
| | Germany | 1 |
| | France | 1 |
| | South Africa | 1 |
| Marital Status | | |
| | Currently Married/Common-law | 11 |
| | Divorced/Separated | 8 |
| | Widowed | 13 |
| | Never Married | 4 |
| Education | | |
| | Less Than High School | 4 |
| | High School | 7 |
| | College/University | 17 |
| | Graduate School | 4 |
| | Technical School | 3 |
| | Other | 1 |
| Household Income | | |
| | Under $10,000 | 1 |
| | $10–20,000 | 2 |
| | $20–30,000 | 5 |
| | $30–40,000 | 7 |
| | $40–50,000 | 6 |
| | $50–60,000 | 2 |
| | $60,000+ | 9 |
| | Declined to Say | 4 |

household income, and marital status, all of the women were heterosexual and most of the women were White and had either been born in Canada or in Western European countries.

## Study #4 Physician Interviews

This study[8] investigated how physicians involved in the delivery of aesthetic medicine perceived non-surgical cosmetic procedures.

Recruited via purposive sampling techniques, a total of eight male physicians (four cosmetic surgeons, two reconstructive plastic surgeons, and two general practitioners) were interviewed. Following a comprehensive search of the directory on the website of the College of Physicians and Surgeons of British Columbia, Canada (https://www.cpsbc.ca/cps), as well as the local telephone book, 47 physicians involved in the aesthetic field in the Greater Vancouver area were identified. These individuals were contacted by mail and invited to participate in the study. The eight individuals who agreed to be interviewed varied in terms of the number and type of non-surgical cosmetic procedures they provided as well as the percentage of their practice that was aesthetically focused and/or devoted to the provision of non-surgical cosmetic procedures. The interview schedule consisted of open-ended questions that asked the physicians to tell the story of how they came to be involved in the field of aesthetic medicine, the type of training that they had pursued and undergone, the centrality of aesthetic procedures (both surgical and non-surgical) to their practices, their descriptions of typical/ideal clients, what they discerned to be their clients' motivations for seeking non-surgical cosmetic procedures, their personal views on the importance of physical attractiveness in later life, and the effectiveness, risks, evolution, and future of non-surgical cosmetic procedures.

## Study #5 Content Analysis of Anti-aging Print Advertisements

The final study[9] entailed a content analysis of anti-aging-related print advertisements that appeared in five women's magazines, namely *Harper's Bazaar, Ladies' Home Journal, More, O: The Oprah Magazine,* and *Vogue,* between July 2004 and July 2005. These magazines were chosen based on their broad appeal to middle-aged and older women as well as their high circulation numbers. Four of the five magazines were ranked among the top 100 revenue-generating magazines by the Magazine Publishers of America (Magazine Publishers of America, 2009). The median readership ages of *Harper's Bazaar, Ladies' Home Journal, More, O: The Oprah Magazine,* and *Vogue* are 38, 55, 51, 46, and 35, respectively. All beauty product advertisements that made reference to anti-aging either with respect to the names of the products or the accompanying text were included in the sample. Both full-page advertisements and pages that consisted of several advertisements placed together were taken into account. Advertisements that were replicated across several issues were included in the analysis, as repetition is a frequently used tool in advertising campaigns (Frith et al., 2005). As a result, a total of 293 advertisements (51 advertisements in *Harper's Bazaar*, 61 advertisements in *Ladies' Home Journal*, 67 advertisements in *More*, 54 advertisements in *Oprah Magazine*, and 60 advertisements in *Vogue*) were collected and analyzed. Two research assistants were hired and trained to independently code the advertisements. A consensus model (Holsti, 1969) was used so that any discrepancies in coding were discussed and decisions were made collectively as to how advertisements should be coded. A code book, which was generated by the intensive reading and rereading of advertisements, included the following broad analytic categories: direct or explicit references to anti-aging, direct or explicit references to non-surgical cosmetic procedures, indirect allusions to non-surgical cosmetic procedures, and products that targeted specific body parts (e.g., face, weight, hair) which had been identified in my previous studies as a focus of women's body dissatisfaction in later life.

## Contextualizing the Narrative Accounts

In order to elucidate the power relations that underlie women's experiences of aging and their perceptions of their bodies, I contextualize the women's narrative accounts by identifying their ages and social class. Using income as a measure of social class and employing Statistics Canada's (2008) concept of low-income cutoffs as a point of reference, I classify the women's annual incomes as falling within the lower class, middle class, or upper class. I consider study participants with household annual incomes under $20,000 to have limited incomes and to fall within the lower class. Similarly, study participants with household annual incomes between $20,000 and $60,000 are referred to as having middle-class incomes. Study participants with household annual incomes above $60,000 are considered affluent or of a higher socioeconomic status. Finally, given that so few of the women in my various samples are lesbian, I only identify a woman's sexual preference when it is other than heterosexual. This is not meant to reinforce heteronormativity but rather to make the descriptors less lengthy.

## STRENGTHS AND LIMITATIONS OF THE STUDIES

One of the most important strengths of this book is the empirical richness that results from the use of data from the five aforementioned studies. Although more than 300 interview hours with 102 women across three distinct studies yields a wealth of nuanced data, the interviews with physicians and the content analysis of print advertisements afford important insights into the cultural context in which women do aging, beauty, and gender (West & Zimmerman, 1987). Elucidating the complexities of and tensions within women's experiences of aging, beauty, and their bodies, the combination of these studies illuminates the poignant and multifaceted realities of living in an anti-aging and appearance-obsessed culture as an older woman. The fact that the studies span a decade also facilitates an examination of emergent attitudes concerning specific aspects of appearance within the context of ever-increasing beauty work options and requirements.

Even as they constitute an important strength, the cohort differences within and between the studies also pose some challenges with respect to comparisons of the data. Similarly, the fact that women in the interview studies are diverse with respect to age, country of origin, educational attainment, ethnicity, income, marital status, race, sexual orientation, and work history allows for analysis of how one's social positioning frames one's experience of ageism and beauty work in later life. However, the majority of women in the interview studies have been White, Canadian born, and heterosexual, and all have been community dwelling. Thus, the experiences of lesbian and queer women, women of color, and frail women who require extensive assistance with activities of daily living are not well represented in the data. In this way, I offer and present the analysis and interpretation of my data as a beginning point for the examination of body image, embodiment, and aging. Where appropriate, I provide detailed descriptors of the women who participated in the study in order to highlight the impact of their social position and the diversity of the samples. Additionally, I tease out potential cohort differences that may exist as a result of social and historical factors.

## NOTES

1. I draw on Calasanti and Slevin's (2001) definition of age relations, which contains three elements: "First, age serves a social organizing principle; second, different age groups gain identities and power in relation to one another; and third, age relations intersect with other power relations" (p. 179).

2. For further details, please see the following articles: L. Hurd Clarke, "Overcoming Ambivalence: The Challenges of Exploring Socially Charged Issues," *Qualitative Health Research* 13, no. 5 (2003): 718–35; L. Hurd Clarke, "Beauty in Later Life: Older Women's Perceptions of Physical Attractiveness," *Canadian Journal on Aging* 21, no. 3 (2002a): 429–42; L. Hurd Clarke, "Older Women's Perceptions of Ideal Body Weights: The Tensions between Health and Appearance Motivations for Weight Loss," *Ageing and Society* 22, no. 6 (2002b): 751–73; L. Hurd Clarke, "Older Women's Bodies and the Self: The Construction of Identity in Later Life," *Canadian Review of Sociology and Anthropology* 38, no. 4 (2001): 441–64; L. Hurd, "Older Women's Body Image and Embodied Experience: An Exploration," *Journal of Women and Aging* 12, no. 3/4 (2000): 77–97.

3. This study was supported by a Social Sciences and Humanities Research Council of Canada Doctoral Fellowship.

4. For further details, please see the following articles: L. Hurd Clarke and M. Griffin, "Body Image and Aging: Older Women and the Embodiment of Trauma," *Women's Studies International Forum* 31, no. 3 (2008a): 200–208; L. Hurd Clarke and M. Griffin, "Visible and Invisible Ageing: Beauty Work as a Response to Ageism," *Ageing and Society* 28, no. 5 (2008b): 653–74; L. Hurd Clarke and M. Griffin, "The Body Natural and the Body Unnatural: Beauty Work and Aging," *Journal of Aging Studies* 21, no. 3 (2007a): 187–201; L. Hurd Clarke and M. Griffin, "Becoming and Being Gendered through the Body: Older Women, Mothers and Body Image," *Ageing and Society* 27, no. 5 (2007b): 701–18; L. Hurd Clarke, R. Repta, and M. Griffin, "Non-surgical Cosmetic Procedures: Older Women's Perceptions and Experiences," *Journal of Women and Aging* 19, no. 3/4 (2007): 69–87.

5. This study was supported by a Social Sciences and Humanities Research Council of Canada Standard Research Grant.

6. For further details, please see the following journal articles: L. Hurd Clarke, M. Griffin, and K. Maliha, "Bat Wings, Bunions, and Turkey Wattles: Body Transgressions and Older Women's Strategic Clothing Choices,"

*Ageing and Society* 29, no. 5 (2009): 709–26; L. Hurd Clarke and A. Bundon, "From 'The Thing To Do' to 'Defying the Ravages of Age': Older Women Reflect on the Use of Lipstick," *Journal of Women and Aging* 21, no. 3 (2009): 198–212; L. Hurd Clarke and A. Korotchenko, "Older Women and Suntanning: The Negotiation of Health and Appearance Risks," *Sociology of Health and Illness* 31, no. 5 (2009): 748–61; L. Hurd Clarke and A. Korotchenko, "Shades of Grey: To Dye or Not to Dye One's Hair in Later Life," *Ageing and Society* 30 (in press).

7. This study was funded by a Michael Smith Foundation for Health Research Establishment Grant and made possible by a Michael Smith Foundation for Health Research Career Scholar Award.

8. This study was also funded by a Michael Smith Foundation for Health Research Establishment Grant and made possible by a Michael Smith Foundation for Health Research Career Scholar Award.

9. This study was funded by a Humanities and Social Sciences Small Grant through the University of British Columbia.

# 2

⚜

# Theorizing the Aging and Aged Woman's Face, Body, and Embodied Experience

Whereas man grows old gradually, woman is suddenly deprived of her femininity; she is still relatively young when she loses the erotic attractiveness and the fertility which, in the view of society and in her own, provide the justification for her existence and her opportunity for happiness. (de Beauvoir, 1949/1952, p. 575)

Articulating the power of cultural discourses pertaining to aging, gender, and femininity on women's experiences of growing older, de Beauvoir was one of the first feminist scholars to tackle the thorny theoretical issue of aging and women's oppression. Since de Beauvoir's magnum opus was published in 1949, there has been a steady, albeit still limited, increase in the theorizing and research concerned with older women's bodies. The literature has tended to focus on three disparate but intrinsically related areas: body image,[1] beauty ideology and the politics of women's bodies, and embodiment[2] and the experience of aging. In this chapter, I examine these literatures[3] in order to situate older women's feelings about and experiences in and through their aging bodies within a Western cultural context that privileges youthfulness, thinness, toned shapeliness, fitness, and healthiness. The chapter sets the stage for a critical examination of older women's body image and embodied experiences of aging in light of the social and physical realities of growing older, which will be discussed in the ensuing chapters.

## WOMEN AND BODY IMAGE

When investigating how women feel about and perceive their bodies, researchers typically use the concept of body image. Defined as "a multidimensional self-attitude toward one's body, particularly its size, shape, and aesthetics" (Cash et al., 1997, p. 433), body image encompasses thoughts, feelings, and perceptions about, as well as investment in, the body. While thoughts, feelings, and perceptions are probed in terms of the individual's assessments of her own body and comparisons with the bodies of others, body image investment is measured in terms of the types of appearance management behaviors and strategies that an individual uses to alter and maintain her appearance (Cash et al., 2004; Muth & Cash, 1997; Striegel-Moore & Franko, 2002). Rather than being fixed, body image is elastic, situational, and the negotiated product of the individual's perceptions and internalization of the cultural beauty ideal, individual body ideal, current body image, actual body shape, and social positioning (Myers & Biocca, 1992; Paquette & Raine, 2004).

The extensive research concerning young and middle-aged women's body image reveals that the majority of women are dissatisfied with their physical appearances, particularly their weight (Bedford & Johnson, 2005; Bordo, 2003; Cash & Henry, 1995; Feingold & Mazzella, 1998; Frost, 2001; Grogan, 2008; McLaren & Kuh, 2004a, 2004b; Pliner et al., 1990; Rodin et al., 1985; Stevens & Tiggemann, 1998; Striegel-Moore & Franko, 2002; Tiggemann & Lynch, 2001). Poor body image and, in particular, women's focus on and dissatisfaction with their weight are so pervasive among women, irrespective of their cultural background, ethnicity, race, sexual preferences, or socioeconomic status, that Rodin et al. (1985) have described it as a normative discontent. Bordo (2003) argues that weight preoccupation is "one of the most powerful normalizing mechanisms of our century, insuring the production of self-monitoring and self-disciplining 'docile bodies'" (p. 186).

The research concerning older women's body image is limited, and there has been relatively little investigation of how older women feel about their aging appearances and bodies (Baker & Gringart, 2009). What is known is that most women gain weight, particularly after menopause, which is accompanied by an increase and redistribution of body fat (Chrisler & Ghiz, 1993). Referring to increases in body weight, changes in fat distribution, and alterations in body shape as a result of sagging skin and the effects of reproduction, Chrisler and Ghiz (1993) assert: "To put it simply, women should expect to change shape as they get older" (p. 69). While little research has investigated women's perceptions and experiences of various bodily changes, the studies that have investigated women's feelings about their weight suggest that it continues to be a key source of body image dissatisfaction in later life (Allaz et al., 1998; Baker & Gringart, 2009; Bedford & Johnson, 2005; Furman, 1997; Hurd, 2000; Slevin, 2006; Tiggemann & Lynch, 2001; Tunaley et al., 1999; Winterich, 2007). Regardless of their age, most women wish to lose weight even when they are of normal weight (Allaz et al., 1998; Henderson-King & Henderson-King, 1997; Hurd Clarke, 2002b). Additionally, the majority of women continually restrict or monitor their caloric intake (Rodin et al., 1985), express a desire for a thinner body shape than they currently possess (Grogan, 2008), and view their bodies with ambivalence, if not targeted displeasure (Bordo, 2003).

## WOMEN AND THE FEMININE BEAUTY IDEAL

The extant research and feminist theorizing suggest that gender relations, as they are enacted through feminine beauty ideals, underlie women's dissatisfaction with their bodies (Bartky, 1998; Bordo, 2003; Rodin, 1992; Wolf, 1991). Women learn from an early age that their social currency largely derives from their ability to achieve and maintain proximity to a privileged feminine appearance, which is a youthful, toned, healthy, voluptuous yet slim body. Since the social opportunities and rewards that women accrue are directly linked to their physical beauty, women are taught to *see* their bodies in particular ways (Bordo, 2003), namely as assemblages of "discrete parts that others aesthetically evaluate" (Franzoi, 1995, p. 417). In particular, women's weight as well as the size and shape of their breasts, buttocks, stomachs, and thighs are the focus of relentless scrutiny (Bartky, 1998; Bordo, 2003; Gimlin, 2002; Grogan, 2008; Wolf, 1991). While men are socialized to value physical strength, prowess, and domination, women are taught to be "insecure bodies, constantly monitoring themselves for signs of imperfection, constantly engaged in physical 'improvement'" (Bordo, 2003, p. 57). In this way, the pursuit of beauty and women's constant "self-surveillance" (Bartky, 1998, p. 42) are forms of patriarchal oppression that simultaneously establish a culturally accepted means of judging and finding women wanting and immobilize women's ability to either individually or collectively resist male dominance (Bartky, 1998; Bordo 2003; Brown & Jasper, 1993; Hesse-Biber, 1996; Seid, 1989).

At the same time, the beauty ideal for women is becoming increasingly elusive. Indeed, contemporary fashion models, beauty pageant contestants, movie stars, and other media icons are far leaner than at any other time in history (Bordo, 2003; Brown & Jasper, 1993; Gimlin, 2002; Hesse-Biber, 1996; Kilbourne, 1994; Rodin et al., 1985; Seid, 1994). Kilbourne (1994) contends that only 5 percent of the female population approximates the extant beauty standard and that the "ideal body type today . . . is unattainable by most women, even if they starve themselves" (p. 396). Thus, the beauty standard is completely disparate from the weights, shapes, and sizes of average women, who are now heavier than at any time previously in history (Spitzer et al., 1999). Given the physical realities of aging, which include the tendency to gain weight over time (Allaz et al., 1998) and the normative increases in body fat deposition, particularly after puberty, pregnancy, and menopause (Chrisler & Ghiz, 1993; Tiggemann & Lynch, 2001), older women are at a particular disadvantage relative to weight and size requirements of the ideal female body.

However, weight reduction is not the only requirement for attaining beauty, as social norms dictate that women must also engage in rigorous exercise to tone and slim the body (Bordo, 2003; Brown & Jasper, 1993; Grogan, 2008; Markula, 1995; Seid, 1989) while simultaneously retaining feminine shapeliness and sexual appeal. The emphasis on being physically fit in order to be beautiful reflects the entrenchment of healthism (Crawford, 1980), which is the cultural norm that individuals are morally obligated to engage in health-promoting activities (White et al., 1995) such as dieting and exercise and thereby take personal responsibility for the health and appearance of their bodies (Oberg & Tornstam, 2001). Within this climate of compulsory, ongoing, and corrective discipline (Foucault, 1979), it is assumed that given willpower and the "right" amount of exercise, diet, beauty aids, and other "investments" such as surgical procedures, gym memberships, and nutritional supplements, the perfect body is attainable by anyone and that all individuals must work toward this goal (Bordo, 2003; Grogan, 2008; Katz, 2000). Failure to look fit and, therefore, healthy and beautiful, indicates that proper discipline and control have not been exercised over the body and that the individual is, at least to some degree, morally bankrupt (Findlay & Miller, 2002; Shilling, 2003).

The final related, and perhaps most restrictive, aspect of the feminine beauty ideal pertains to age. Within Western contemporary culture, physical beauty is assumed to be a resource only available to the young, and old bodies, particularly elderly female bodies, are perceived to be ugly, repulsive, asexual, and undesirable (Calasanti & Slevin, 2001; Cruikshank, 2003; Furman, 1997; Holstein, 2006; Hurd, 1999; Wolf, 1991). Women are strongly encouraged to engage in various kinds of beauty work in order to "look younger and hence 'better'" (Furman, 1997, p. 117). From makeup and hair dye to surgical and non-surgical cosmetic alterations, the range of beauty products and services available to women is seemingly endless. Additionally, beauty work has become synonymous with the practice of dieting and exercise, as well as various other strategies to decrease and control one's body weight and size. Noting that the ideal female body has become progressively more youthful, Seid (1989) asserts that the contemporary societal obsession with being thin and toned has arisen from the prevailing cultural belief that thinness and youthfulness are indistinguishable. Thus, individuals discipline the body through exercise, dieting, and adherence to the latest ideas pertaining to healthy living not only to be physically fit, and, therefore, beautiful, but also to approximate the cultural idealization and endless pursuit of youth.

## BEAUTY IDEOLOGY AND SOCIAL POSITIONING

While the young, thin, toned, yet curvy feminine beauty ideal is pervasive, not all women have identical body images or uniformly embrace extant Western constructs of beauty as they are portrayed in and disseminated by the media. Rather, body image and internalized beauty ideals reflect a negotiation between individuals' sociopolitical, cultural, and historical positioning, and emergent social norms. Black and Sharma (2001) argue that "there is room for tension and ambiguity within femininity" (p. 102) as the internalization of the feminine beauty ideal varies by age, class, ethnicity, sexual orientation, and women's own "gender attitudes and ideologies" (Cash et al., 1997, p. 433). In this way, each woman holds a particular idealized beauty standard which is culturally and historically situated and against which she measures her own appearance successes and failures.

To begin, the beauty ideals of older women differ from those of their younger counterparts in several key respects. Some researchers have found that while appearance work is a lifelong requirement of doing femininity (West & Zimmerman, 1987), women's attention to their looks decreases with age as the functionality of the body becomes a source of increasing concern in the face of the loss of functional abilities and the onset of health issues (Franzoi & Koehler, 1998; Hurd, 2000; Pliner et al., 1990; Reboussin et al., 2000). In other words, a woman's priorities with respect to her body shift when her abilities to live independently or engage in valued activities are threatened. Interestingly, Baker and Gringart's (2009) recent study revealed that although women become more health conscious as they age, and, therefore, more concerned with the physical functioning of their bodies, they also devote progressively more time to beauty work as they struggle to counteract the effects of physical aging on their appearances. Therefore, Baker and Gringart's (2009) research suggests that growing awareness of the importance of the functionality of the body in later life does not erase or even minimize older women's concerns for their appearances.

At the same time, other research has demonstrated that older women prefer more curvaceous and heavier figures than their younger female counterparts who are more likely to privilege thinness as an indicator of physical attractiveness (Hurd Clarke, 2002a; Lamb et al., 1993). However, Hallinan and Schuler (1993) report that like younger women, older women tend to have an ideal body shape that is considerably smaller than what they themselves have, suggesting that negative evaluations of one's body shape, size, and weight persist into older age. Echoing these findings, my research (Hurd Clarke, 2002b) has further indicated that older women are dissatisfied with their weight and that the majority either currently practice or have, at one point in time, practiced weight control or weight reduction strategies. Similarly, Slevin (2006) has found that older lesbian women experienced their weight as an ongoing source of dissatisfaction requiring disciplinary vigilance.

Additionally, research suggests that the beauty ideals to which women subscribe are associated with their social class. Women of higher socioeconomic status have been found to be more dissatisfied with or concerned about their physical appearances, particularly their weight, than women of lower socioeconomic status (McLaren & Kuh, 2004b; Ogden & Thomas, 1999; Wardle & Griffith, 2001). Abell and Richards (1996) note that there is a stronger relationship between body shape satisfaction and self-esteem among upper-class women as compared to lower-class women. Reflecting the links between increased education and concomitant health knowledge and the internalization of healthist norms that hold individuals morally responsible for the status of their bodies, McLaren and Kuh (2004b) report that body dissatisfaction is most strongly tied to the attainment of high levels of education. Further elucidating the relationship between class and body image and using Bourdieu's concept of habitus, Dumas, Laberge, and Straka (2005) found that working-class older women placed less emphasis on appearance than upper-class older women because economic hardship presented them with more pressing issues than the concern for physical attractiveness. In contrast, affluent older women tended to be more dissatisfied with their appearances and to engage in a wide variety of appearance-enhancing practices. However, over time both working class and affluent older women in their study reevaluated their conceptions of beauty and the importance of youthfulness as they began to emphasize personality and character over appearance.

The extant research also reveals that different cultural and racial groups hold divergent beauty ideals and varying degrees of body image satisfaction. For example, Hesse-Biber, Howling, Leavy, and Lovejoy (2004) note that body image dissatisfaction among young African American women is linked more to hair quality and skin color than to weight. Other studies have also found that African American women resist the extremes of thinness embodied in the White beauty ideal (Hesse-Biber et al., 2004; Molloy & Herzberger, 1998). Although they tend to express dissatisfaction with their weight and general appearances (Thomas & James, 1988), African American women are often less concerned about dieting and thinness and more likely to hold more positive attitudes toward being overweight and obese (Harris et al., 1991) than their White counterparts. Some studies further suggest that African American women prefer to be slightly overweight rather than slightly underweight (Hesse-Biber et al., 2004; Molloy & Herzberger, 1998). Molloy and Herzberger (1998) report that the resistance of dominant constructions of feminine beauty are linked to differing cultural beauty ideals as well as to perceptions of what African American males prefer. Hesse-Biber et al. (2004) argue that the possession of a strong sense of racial identity may serve to protect some African American young women from body image dissatisfaction by enabling them to "operate outside of White norms of beauty, focusing not on weight, but on character and presentation as integral aspects of one's beauty" (p. 73).

The research concerning the body image of Asian women has produced conflicting results. Some studies have suggested that Asian women have a more positive body image than Hispanic, African American, or White women (see, for example, Altabe, 1998; Cachelin et al., 2002; Molloy & Herzberger, 1998). A number of studies also have found lower rates of disordered eating among Asian women as compared to White women (Akan & Grilo, 1995; Ratan et al., 1998). In contrast, Sussman, Truong, and Lim's (2007) survey of 353 immigrant women revealed that Chinese immigrant women had the poorest body image while Afro-Caribbean immigrant women viewed their bodies the most positively. Sussman et al. (2007) also found that acculturation correlated with more positive body image among their

Asian immigrant women participants. Surveying a diverse sample of college-aged women, Forbes and Frederick (2008) found that Asian women had the lowest body image satisfaction and the greatest dissatisfaction with their breast sizes as compared to White, Hispanic, and African women. Yates, Edman, and Aruguete (2004) found that Chinese females were highly satisfied with their bodies whereas Japanese females were highly dissatisfied, underscoring the importance of attending to the cultural complexities subsumed under and homogenized by the use of the broad term Asian.

The research is divided as to how influential sexual preference is for women's body image and body satisfaction. Some research has suggested that lesbians are less dissatisfied with their bodies and appearances than heterosexual women (Bergeron & Senn, 1998; Herzog et al., 1992; Siever, 1994; Winterich, 2007). Pointing to alternative beauty standards within the lesbian community, researchers have suggested that lesbian women are buffered from the negative influences of conventional norms of physical attractiveness that tend to cause women to feel poorly about their appearances (Bergeron & Senn, 1998; Brown, 1987; Pitman, 2000; Taub, 2003; Winterich, 2007). However, other research indicates that body image dissatisfaction among lesbian women is comparable to that of heterosexual women (Berenet et al., 1996; Brand et al., 1992; Cogan, 1999; Dworkin, 1989; Slevin, 2006; Striegel-Moore et al., 1990). This research suggests that gender and gender socialization are more determinative of body image dissatisfaction than is sexual orientation.

Finally, differences in the beauty ideals held by women have been examined in terms of ideological orientation. The literature indicates that adherence to a feminist identity and/or feminist ideology (as compared with traditional views of femininity) is not associated with more favorable body image (Cash et al., 1997; Dionne et al., 1995). Rather, Cash et al. (1997) found that the explanatory factor for differences in body image satisfaction across groups of women was linked to the internalization of "conventional expectations and preferences about gender roles in male-female social relations" (p. 441). Cash et al. (1997) state that their findings suggest that "messages about the importance of women's appearance, both in general and in developing and maintaining intimate relationships with men, may be so ingrained and socially reinforced that the acquisition of feminist ideology has little impact on these core beliefs" (p. 442).

In summary, body image and beauty ideology are socially situated such that age, culture, gender identity, sexual preference, and socioeconomic status influence women's feelings about their bodies and their definitions of female attractiveness. Despite the differences across social positions, the research suggests dissatisfaction with appearance is pervasive among younger women whose feelings about themselves as individuals, their perceived social worth, and their attitudes toward their bodies are shaped in deleterious ways by patriarchal beauty ideology. However, there continues to be limited understanding and exploration of how beauty ideologies influence the experiences and attitudes of older women.

## AGEISM AND BEAUTY IDEOLOGY

By virtue of its emphasis on youthfulness, the extant beauty ideal embodies and exacerbates ageist assumptions and interpretations of the aging female body. A term originally coined by Robert Butler in 1969, *ageism* is "a set of social relations that discriminate against older people and set them apart as being different by defining and understanding them in an oversimplified, generalized way" (Minichiello et al., 2000, p. 253). Bytheway (1995) states that "ageism legitimates the use of chronological age to mark out classes of people who are systematically denied resources and opportunities that others enjoy, and who suffer the consequences of such denigration, ranging from well-meaning patronage to unambiguous vilification" (p. 14). Thus, ageism is manifested in numerous ways, including "1) Prejudicial attitudes toward the aged, toward old age, and toward the aging process . . . 2) discriminatory practices against the elderly . . . and 3) institutional practices and policies which . . . perpetuate stereotypic beliefs about the elderly, reduce their opportunities . . . and undermine their personal dignity" (Butler, 1980, p. 8). In this way, ageism involves age relations which are "ones of privilege and oppression"

(Calasanti, 2007, p. 336), whereby the young accrue power, social currency, and resources at the expense of the old and deem their advantageous position within the social hierarchy to be rightful, "'natural' and beyond dispute" (Calasanti, 2007, p. 336). Moreover, Laws (1995) notes that "ageism    is an embodied form of oppression" (p. 114) that entails the construction and internalization of oppression toward and through bodies.

While ageism can be subtle, as in the case of birthday cards, which often rely on negative stereotypes of old age and old bodies as a source of humor (Bytheway, 1995; Demos & Jache, 1981; Dillon & Jones, 1981; Gibson, 1993), it can also be overt, as in the case of age-based workplace discrimination and mandatory retirement (Barnett, 2005; Bendick et al., 1996; Berger, 2006; Chiu et al., 2001; Laws, 1995; McCann & Giles, 2002; McMullin & Marshall, 2001; Taylor & Walker, 1998; Walker et al., 2007) or the built environment (Laws, 1995). Other examples of ageism that have been researched include the negative stereotypes held by the young and old alike (Cuddy et al., 2005; Hurd, 1999; Kite & Wagner, 2002; Minichiello et al., 2000), humor (Bowd, 2003; Bytheway, 1995; Palmore, 1999), and poor treatment of older adults by health care providers (Adams et al., 2006; Gott et al., 2004; Greene et al., 1996; Kane & Kane, 2005; McCormack, 2002; Nelson, 2005).

Some scholars have argued that ageism facilitates the construction of "a culture that discards old people" (Siegal, 1992, p. 55) through the establishment and reinforcement of cultural ideals that privilege youthfulness and independence as indicators of normality (Hennessy, 1989). Ageism allows younger adults to dehumanize older adults and view older generations as a social category, a social problem, an "other" (Canales, 2000), and an example of deviance from normalcy (Arber & Ginn, 1991a, 1991b; Quadagno, 1999). Healey (1993) aptly states: "the basic assumption underlying ageism . . . [is] that youth is good, desirable, and beautiful; old age is bad, repulsive, and ugly" (p. 48). Old age is thereby an undesirable condition, which must be fought at all costs and with all available means because "we are judged not on the basis of how old we are but on how young we are not" (Secunda, 1984, p. 2).

While ageism is a powerful force that drives consumer culture, influences everyday social interactions, and underscores extant social policies affecting all older adults, older women are particularly at risk of societal discrimination and prejudicial treatment (Calasanti & Slevin, 2001; Cruikshank, 2003; Ginn & Arber, 1995). Older women are subject to negative stereotyping and discriminatory behavior by virtue of their simultaneous membership in the categories of "old" and "woman" with the resultant combined impact of ageism and sexism (Arber & Ginn, 1991a). Thus, older women are among the most devalued and marginalized social groups. The extant literature is replete with examples of "gendered ageism" (Ginn & Arber, 1995, p. 7) in the workplace (Duncan & Loretto, 2004; Itzin & Phillipson, 1995; McMullin & Berger, 2006; Walker et al., 2007) and with regard to pensions and retirement (Calasanti & Slevin, 2001; Ginn & Arber, 1993, 1996). Indeed, women are more likely than men to experience age discrimination as a result of their appearances (Duncan & Loretto, 2004; Walker et al., 2007). Women also have a greater likelihood of trying to appear as youthful as possible in order to defend against age stereotyping (Itzin & Phillipson, 1995). Despite their efforts, women tend to be perceived as being older than their same-aged male counterparts by employers and managers and they achieve peak earnings at a younger age than men (Duncan & Loretto, 2004; Itzin & Phillipson, 1993). Consequently, women are economically disadvantaged in later life as they have fewer financial resources relative to their older male partners (Barnett, 2005; Duncan & Loretto, 2004; Falkingham & Rake, 1999; Ginn & Arber, 1993).

Unlike the research concerning the social structural discrimination against older women, there has been limited theorizing regarding the impact of gendered ageism on societal evaluations of older women's bodies and aging female appearances. As many other scholars have noted, the notion of a double standard of aging, namely the idea that signs of aging in a woman's physical appearance are frequently reviled while similar changes in men are revered and even considered sexy, has become a truism. Men have two standards of attractiveness available to them, namely the young Adonis (Lorber & Moore, 2007) or the distinguished older man (Lee, 1998), whereas definitions of beauty for women are solely linked to youthfulness (Cruikshank,

2003; Calasanti & Slevin, 2001; Halliwell & Dittmar, 2003). Moreover, women are deemed to be old, and therefore to have failed at beauty (Holstein, 2006), at a much younger age than men (Calasanti, 2005; Calasanti & Slevin, 2001; Ginn & Arber, 1995; Lee, 1998; Woodward, 1999a). Given the centrality of appearance to women's social currency and the successful doing of femininity, failing at beauty has dire consequences for older women, who face cultural irrelevance and social invisibility (Calasanti, 2005; Hurd Clarke & Griffin, 2008a; Twigg, 2004). Summarizing the devastating impact of looking and being old for women, McPherson (1990) has stated that the aging process "enhances a man but progressively destroys a woman" (p. 243). Thus, although variation exists by social status, women are confronted with intense social pressure to fight the physical signs of aging and to preserve youthful appearances so as to stave off age-based discrimination and social disparagement (Holstein, 2006; Hurd Clarke & Griffin, 2008a; Wolf, 1991).

## OLDER WOMEN AND EMBODIMENT

In addition to body image and the interrogation of beauty ideology, sociocultural researchers have employed the concept of embodiment to investigate and analyze women's everyday life. Referring to individuals' experiences within and through their bodies, the term *embodiment* originates from the work of Merleau-Ponty (1962) and Strauss (1963) and their conceptualization of the "lived body" (Lash, 1991; Leder, 1984; Young, 1990). Turner (1984) summarizes the concept of embodiment in this way: "There is an obvious and prominent fact about human beings: They have bodies and they are bodies. More lucidly, human beings are embodied, just as they are enselved" (p. 1). Similarly, Nettleton and Watson (1998) assert that embodied experience, or the lived body, refers to "the body as it is experienced by human beings, who both *have* and *are* bodies" (p. 2, emphasis in original). Rather than adhering to Cartesian notions of mind-body dualism and the resultant "fragmentation of the body into a series of body-parts in consumer culture" (Featherstone & Turner, 1995, p. 1), embodiment conceptualizes the body as both subject and object (Crossley, 1995;

Merleau-Ponty, 1962) and refers to the ways in which behavior, emotions, identity, meanings, and society are constructed through the doings of the body (Crossley, 1995).

Research on women's embodiment has explored such topics as: the "breasted experiences of women" (Millsted & Frith, 2003, p. 455; Lee, 1997), the experience of having breast cancer (Lende & Lachiondo, 2009; Thomas-MacLean, 2005), being pregnant (Earle, 2003; Lupton, 1999; Young, 1984), breast-feeding (Dykes, 2005; Schmied & Barclay, 1999; Schmied & Lupton, 2001), having cosmetic surgery (Davis, 1995, 2003), and reaching menarche (Lee, 2009; Lee & Sasser-Coen, 1996). Additionally, the research has investigated the commodification of gender and sexuality in the example of female exotic dancers (Rambo et al., 2006), the construction of the embodiment of femininity among female flight attendants (Tyler & Hancock, 2001), the midlife woman's experience of menopause (Ballard et al., 2009; Boughton, 2002; Dillaway, 2005a, 2005b; Fairhurst, 1998; Mackey, 2007; Morris & Symonds, 2004; Perz & Ussher, 2008), and transgressions in gendered embodiment such as in the case of professional female football players (Kotarba & Held, 2006) and body building (Johnston, 1996). Collectively, this research has revealed that the body is deeply intertwined with an individual's construction and experience of identity, femininity, sexuality, and the "doing of gender" (West & Zimmerman, 1987) as well as the site of women's ongoing "surveillance and control, both on the part of the women themselves and of others" (Lupton, 1999, p. 60). Rather than being an innate or ascribed personal characteristic, gender is an "accomplishment" that is constructed through embodied behavior that conforms to "normative conceptions of femininity or masculinity" (West & Zimmerman, 1987, p. 136). As well as being "performed" in and through bodies via behavior, speech patterns, and gestures (Butler, 1990), the doing of gender involves the negotiation of the gendered social and cultural meanings that are attributed to bodies and body parts, such as breasts (Millsted & Frith, 2003), and that underscore women's societal oppression.

Although Laz (2003) has argued that appearance is one of the four key aspects of aged embodiment (which also include activity, fitness, and health; energy; and ailments and illness), little attention has been given to older women's experiences in the domain of embodiment research. Indeed, the research concerning embodiment in later life has been largely focused on health and illness experiences, particularly those related to topics such as frailty (Grenier & Hanley, 2007) and the management of the aging body, such as in the case of Twigg's (1997) excellent study concerning bathing. Additionally, there is a wealth of research examining the experience of having particular chronic health conditions like arthritis (Bury, 1988; Rosenfeld & Faircloth, 2004), Alzheimer's disease and dementia (Kontos, 2004; Phinney & Chesla, 2003), effects of stroke (Becker & Kaufman, 1995; Faircloth et al., 2004), osteoarthritis (Sanders et al., 2002), osteoporosis (Roberto, 1990; Wilkins, 2001), and rheumatoid arthritis (Bury, 1982). This research suggests that the body is an "absent presence" (Leder, 1990, p. 13) that "remains largely unproblematic and taken for granted" (Williams, 1996, p. 24) until the onset of illness or some other crisis brings the physical reality of the body into the conscious awareness of the individual. Bury (1982) contends that illness often results in a "biographical disruption" (p. 167) and the perception of "body failure" (Corbin & Strauss, 1988, p. 49), which fractures the individual's sense of embodied identity (Bury, 1982; Charmaz, 1995; Corbin & Strauss, 1988). In other words, the experience of pain, disability, and loss of functional abilities makes the individual more cognizant of both the physical, objective body and the experienced, subjective body. Negative body experiences such as pain and the loss of functional abilities force reevaluations of taken-for-granted assumptions about the nature, potential, reliability, and future of the body. These reappraisals of the embodied self take place in a social context that emphasizes health, ability, independence, and youth and which thereby constructs illness as a form of stigmatized social deviance (Goffman, 1963). In this way, the embodiment literature tends to focus on how physical losses and changes are implicated in the construction and maintenance of the embodied self or identity.

The research concerning older women's experiences of sexuality is one notable exception to the tendency of scholars to ignore later-life-gendered embodiment. Although the existing research has indicated that sexual activity, sexual satisfaction (especially for women), and passionate love decline in later life as a result of the loss of novelty or the onset of health issues (Carpenter et al., 2006; Connidis, 2006), age has been found to predict rates of sexual activity but not levels of sexual desire (Kontula & Haavio-Mannila, 2009). There have been several studies which have explored the meanings and importance that older women attribute to sexual activity and sexuality (Gott & Hinchliff, 2003; Hinchliff & Gott, 2008; Hurd Clarke, 2006). This research has illuminated how older women tend to define sexual activity in broad terms (Hinchliff & Gott, 2008; Hurd Clarke, 2006) and that they place greater emphasis on companionship, cuddling, and affection than they do on sexual intercourse. Contrary to the stereotype of the asexual older adult, this research indicates that sex is important to many older women, particularly those who have partners (Gott & Hinchliff, 2003).

## MEDICALIZATION AND THE AGING FEMALE BODY

As well as being embodied and shaped by sociocultural meanings pertaining to aging and femininity, older women's experiences of growing older have been strongly influenced by medicalization. Riessman (1998) contends that medicalization involves two interconnected processes:

> First, certain behaviours or conditions are given medical meaning—that is, defined in terms of health and illness. Second, medical practice becomes a vehicle for eliminating or controlling problematic experiences that are defined as deviant. (pp. 47–48)

Medicalization has defined aging and aged appearances as health issues in need of medical intervention. For example, the development of hormone replacement therapy in the 1960s resulted in menopause being constructed as a "hormonal deficiency disease" in the United States (Freund et al., 2003; Harding, 1997; Kaufert, 1982). In contrast, feminists have argued that menopause is a natural part of the aging process (Dillaway, 2005a; Martin, 1987) and the extant research suggests that women's personal experience of menopause is shaped by their sociocultural context (Dillaway, 2007; Freund et al., 2003). Similarly, the development of cosmetic surgery and aesthetic medicine culminated in the medicalization of appearance whereby bodily struc-tures that deviated from cultural beauty ideals, including wrinkles or evidence of past pregnancies such as enlarged stomachs and sagging breasts, could be surgically erased from the female body (Davis, 1995; Fraser, 2003, Gibson. 2006; Wolf, 1991) More recently, the introduc tion of non-surgical cosmetic procedures has expanded the range and financial accessibility of beauty options available to women in their fight against aging, especially wrinkles, with a profound impact on the way that older women view and respond to their facial creases, as will be discussed in chapter 4.

## THEORETICALLY SITUATING THIS BOOK

In summary, to fully understand how older women experience and perceive their bodies, it is important to attend to body image, em-bodied experience, and beauty ideology. Blood (2005) has asserted that rather than quantifying women's perceptions of their body sizes and shapes, body image research needs to examine "the cultivation of 'inner' bodily awareness" (p. 125) in relation to women's thoughts and feelings in and about their bodies. She therefore calls for an in-vestigation of the "meanings and emotional states women attribute to different body sizes" (Blood, 2005, p. 125). Similarly, Gubrium and Holstein (2003) have contended that the body is not a static compila-tion of body parts but is rather "an unfinished experiential entity" (p. 205) that is continually interpreted and reinterpreted in social inter-actions. Instead of being "a material entity with physical presence" (Gubrium & Holstein, 2003, pp. 206–7), the body is subjective, situ-ated in everyday life, and "a material entity suffused with meaning" (Gubrium & Holstein, 2003, p. 207). Thus, any exploration of older women's bodies must attend to both their experiences in and through their aging bodies as well as the meanings, thoughts, and feelings that they attribute to their bodies. Further, to understand perceptions of and lived experiences in the body, one must examine the sociocultural context in which these perceptions and experiences are constructed and negotiated. Specifically, it is important to situate an analysis of older women's bodies in the context of cultural understandings of aging, beauty, femininity, and gender as well as the physical realities of growing older. Just as "women's breasts are invested with social, cultural, and political meanings which shape the ways in which we make sense of and experience our embodied selves" (Millsted & Frith, 2003, p. 455), so too are older women's bodies, particularly their wrinkles, gray hair, sagging skin, and other visible signs of aging, imbued with powerful meanings.

Some feminists contend that women have limited agency in a society that defines female value according to appearance and renders them constantly insecure and lacking (Bartky, 1998; Bordo, 2003, 2009; Hesse-Biber, 1996; Seid, 1994). Other feminists suggest that women may find the act of attending to or even altering their appearances to be liberating and empowering as well as creative and pleasurable (Beausoleil, 1994; Davis, 1997; Gimlin, 2000; Negrin, 2002; Weitz, 2001). I maintain that while women exercise agency through their adherence to or resistance of norms of physical beauty, the beauty work behaviors they decide to engage in, the emphasis they place on appearance, and the degree to which their identities are tied to their bodies and social assessments of their appearances are constrained within a determining social context that is framed by patriarchal and ageist cultural norms pertaining to femininity, older women, and physical appearance. Additionally, some women are more constrained than others by virtue of their social, historical, and cultural positioning. The decision to resist cultural norms of femininity and female beauty puts women, particularly older women, at risk of losing social currency and being rendered invisible. In this way, the examination of embodied appearance in later life provides a potent means of investigating the lived realities of ageism and sexism as they are written on and through older women's bodies.

# 3

⌒⌒

# Embodied Appearance in Later Life: What Older Women Have to Say

Old age is no place for sissies.

—Bette Davis

In the 1950 award-winning movie *All about Eve,* Bette Davis plays an aging movie star, Margo Channing, whose Broadway career is upstaged, if not stolen, by a young, conniving woman named Eve who ingratiates herself into the lives of Margo and her friends. Davis's gritty portrayal masterfully delivers insights into how women experience the loss of idealized beauty, the impact and nature of age relations, and the physical realities of growing old in a youth- and beauty-obsessed society. For example, Margo expresses fear about her longtime partner leaving her for the "young and so fair" Eve, alludes to concerns about her weight in relation to a girdle that she suggests is shrinking, describes her own body as a corpse that has not been completely embalmed, bemoans the fact that she is now over 40, rails against the double standard of aging, and conveys a powerful emotional rawness evoked by her gradual yet relentless obsolescence.

While there have been a few Hollywood movies such as *All about Eve* concerning older women's experiences of growing older, the scholarly research giving voice to older women has been noticeably limited. In this chapter, I examine how older women describe their bodies and the physical signs of aging, including their attitudes toward weight gain, gray hair, and changes in physical abilities. While I mention attitudes toward wrinkles, this topic is covered more fully in the next chapter, where I focus on anti-aging beauty work and aesthetic medicine. Examining the complex and often contradictory meanings that older women attribute to their aging bodies, the present chapter explicates how many older women's appearance priorities shift with the onset of health problems in later life as well as how their negative self-evaluations are tempered by pragmatic assertions about the physical and social realities of growing older. I conclude the chapter with a discussion of the data in light of age relations and feminist theorizing on the body.

## OLDER WOMEN, AGING BODIES, AND BODY IMAGE

When asked directly about their feelings about their bodies and/or the appearances of other older women, the majority of the female study participants that I have interviewed over the past decade, irrespective of their ages, educational attainment, incomes, marital or partner statuses, and sexual preferences, and like their younger counterparts (see, for example, Bedford & Johnson, 2005; Bordo, 2003; Cash & Henry, 1995; Feingold & Mazzella, 1998; Grogan, 2008; McLaren & Kuh, 2004a, 2004b; Pliner et al., 1990; Rodin et al., 1985; Stevens & Tiggemann, 1998; Striegel-Moore & Franko, 2002; Tiggemann & Lynch, 2001), have tended to suggest that older women's appearances are unappealing and certainly not the epitome of female beauty. During the past 10 years I have frequently encountered women who have tended to describe the typical older woman's body with words such as "awful," "a disaster," "dumpy," "droopy," "fat," "sagging," "ugh," "ugly," and "yuck" (see Hurd, 2000, for further details). For example, an 82-year-old, upper-class woman contended: "The aging body is a disaster. No question about it. As far as appearance is concerned, it's ugly." Similarly, the women have used words like "awful," "bagged out," "disgusting," "disappointing," "horrifying," "terrible," and "shocking" to describe their own bodies. An 88-year-old woman who had a limited income summarized her assessment of the aging female body as follows:

> No one wants to get old. It's the saddest thing that can happen to anybody besides dying. . . . When you're young, your body's pretty and your feet are pretty. . . . When you get older, your body will change—your body is not pretty anymore. . . . Nobody elderly has got a nice figure. I don't know what happens to it. We just fall apart, I think.

Some women suggested that the equation of beauty with youthfulness was a fact of nature, as expressed by a 65-year-old, middle-class woman:

> The younger of any species is more attractive than the older ones. You know, even animals and fish and birds because the hair or the feathers are shinier and, therefore, prettier. The flesh, whether it's an animal or a person, is firmer. I think that generally looks prettier than saggy. Also, the eyes are brighter and the teeth are healthier-looking. That's life. You know, just, that's just the way it goes.

Queries about their favorite physical features have often left the women stymied. In addition to being met with incredulous looks, awkward laughs, or puzzled silences, I have frequently received terse responses as the women struggled to identify or elaborate upon aspects of their appearances of which they were fond. Only 11 of the 22 women in my first set of interviews with older women were eventually able to identify something positive, as three women stated that they liked their smiles, four indicated that they liked their eyes, and four women named a particular body part or physical function, including their legs (two women), the abilities of her hands (one woman), and the capacities of her brain (one woman). In contrast, 11 women were unable to name any feature that they felt good about either because they had never given it any thought (three women) or, more commonly, because the things they had most admired about their appearances were no longer a source of pleasure due to the physical changes that had occurred over time (eight women).

Interestingly, in my subsequent research with women aged 50 to 70, I found that the younger women in the sample were more easily able to identify aspects of their bodies that they esteemed. Although the women who were pleased with their bodies were in a very small minority, their comments were very revealing. For example, a 56-year-old, middle-class woman stated:

> My favorite thing about my body is my breasts probably. I have really great breasts and I've always had really great breasts and every man I've been with has said, "God you've got great breasts!" . . . I've always gotten absolutely positive feedback from men. And interestingly enough even though my breasts might be my best feature at least three of the significant relationships have—they really liked my bum because I've got this cute little bum. So I've always had tremendously positive feedback from all the men in my life about my body. Hence my self-confidence at 56. . . . I'm real happy with my body. . . . How many people at 56 can say they still turn men's heads, you know? So, hey, what the hell!

Thus, the relatively unchanged body combined with the ability to retain the male gaze by virtue of it was an important determinant of the woman's positive body image.

Similarly, there has been a small group of women who have described an ongoing ambivalent struggle with their bodies, as they moved between acceptance, if not appreciation, of their appearances and self-loathing. A 65-year-old, middle-class woman who described herself as a feminist put it this way:

> I vacillate. I do so much vacillating. There are days when I feel okay about my body because in some ways, my body is still slim and therefore it is okay. But other days I feel repulsed by my own body, because it's old and it's not the way the media is demanding that it be. . . . I would like to think there are women out there who haven't bought into these horrible values.

Echoing Myers and Biocca's (1992) concept of body image as elastic and situational, such women have described an uneasy relationship with their bodies that is influenced by the media, significant others, and their own shifting perceptions and attitudes.

Perhaps not surprising given the way that women are taught to ruthlessly and endlessly scrutinize and critique their bodies (Bartky, 1998; Bordo, 2003), the rejoinders to requests for information about sources of appearance displeasure were often lengthy and numerous. Some women even used the question about satisfaction with their physical features to begin to enumerate their perceived physical faults. Other women introduced the topic of perceived appearance failings in the midst of discussions of unrelated issues. Regardless of when the women chose to reflect on what they did not like about their appearances, their comments were often harsh and extensive. For example, a 73-year-old woman who had a very limited income stated:

> I hate my hands. I hate my feet. I hate my belly. I hate my bum. I hate my boobs. So, now there's nothing—I don't really like anything. I used to like it because I thought I was fairly tall . . . but now, I don't think there's any part of my body that I like. . . . I always look in the mirror and think I look horrible. . . . I don't like my body.

The most commonly noted physical flaws were, in order of frequency, stomachs, legs, breasts, and arms. Thus, a 67-year-old, lower-class woman had this to say:

> I think it's the stomach that bothers me more than the sagging breasts. . . . I mean, when you wear a bra, it doesn't look too bad but this stomach really bothers me. When I was younger I had a very flat tummy. Even after my son was born within six months I was back to more or less normal. But boy this stomach!

Similarly, a 73-year-old, middle-class woman reported:

> I don't think my legs are attractive. I don't think they look nice. I don't think they're good to look at. I read a story once and this kid . . . grew up in an old folks' home . . . and he said he felt he grew up in "a sea of blue veins" because he was down below and only looking at these legs. . . . I don't want to inflict that on anybody. . . . At my age, your body looks as if it's breaking down to me. I don't like wearing really low neck things anymore and my arms are not as firm anymore. So I don't like wearing strappy shirts because my arms have little floppy things underneath even though I exercise and I have all these wrinkles [pointing to her neck and chest].

A 62-year-old woman who had a very limited income directed her displeasure toward her arms:

> I get so disgusted when I see what age has done to my body. Like, I'll put on a tank top or a halter top and then I see bulges where I used to have muscle tone in my arms—now I've got wrinkles on my arms!

In addition to identifying things that they were displeased with, many women juxtaposed what they considered to be their bodily transgressions against the cultural beauty ideal[1] and the perceived appraisals of men. For example, an 87-year-old, upper-class woman had this to say:

> Women's bodies are ugly—older women's bodies. . . . I think most people think their bodies are ugly. . . . Even women before 60. Once they start to sag and stuff, there's no beauty in it. If you're looking for beauty as . . . in the bodies we see on TV, all these lovely, gorgeous girls—if that's beauty, then women over 50 or 60 whose bodies are sagging, their busts are sagging, their bellies are all over, you know, from the baby bearing, and the ass is sagging—they're ugly. There's no beauty in that. No man is going find beauty in that.

Once again, the women reiterated the importance of male attention and sexual interest as an indicator of feminine attractiveness. Some of the women also emphasized the ability of older men to continue to achieve physical attractiveness in contrast to the increasing demerits associated with an aged female body. For example, a 67-year-old, middle-class woman asserted:

> It seems to be a physical fact that many men improve with age whereas women usually don't. . . . Maybe men's faces are stronger to begin with so they can take more lines and crags and that sort of thing. It adds to their features rather than detracts the way it does with a woman's more delicate features.

Although this woman, like most of the other women I interviewed, accepted with certainty the disparities between the meanings attributed to older male and female bodies, a few women suggested that the "double standard" (Sontag, 1972) of aging for male and female appearances was inequitable, as expressed by a 61-year-old woman of lower income status: "It's not a fair society. Older men, when they're 60 and get the grayish hair, they're still looking good. You know, they look sophisticated and downright sexy. But not all women can look that way." However, although this woman allowed for the possibility that women might be deemed attractive in later life, she was unable to reconcile that perception with her strong dissatisfaction with her own aging physical features. In this way, she, like the majority of other women in the three studies, suggested that beauty was increasingly unobtainable for the aging female body as she accepted ageist and sexist beauty ideals despite their perceived inequities.

## THE POWER OF THE REFLECTED IMAGE

In addition to viewing the aging appearance negatively, many older women compared their current bodies with younger, idealized bodies and thereby found their own current appearances sorely wanting. Specifically, study participants often expressed the sense that time was slowly stealing what beauty remained from their aging appearances. For example, a 59-year-old woman who had a lower-class income and who had previously used Restylane to address the physical signs of aging and her dissatisfaction with her appearance had this to say:

> I can see it when I look in the mirror. I know I'm old. . . . I can see the wrinkles coming. That's probably why it bothers me so much to look in the mirror and see myself growing older because I was always fairly attractive as a young woman. . . . I hate getting old. I absolutely hate it. . . . When I look in the mirror, like after being young and fairly attractive for most of my life and getting a fair amount of attention because of that, it's really deflating to watch yourself grow old.

As expressed in the above quotation, the women had internalized ageist discourses that equated physical attractiveness with youthfulness and concomitant perceptions of aged appearances as being devalued and unappealing. The acceptance of these discourses served to undermine their self-esteem and sense of well-being and led to strong feelings of antipathy toward growing older. Indeed, many women expressed dismay and sometimes even self-loathing as a result of the physical changes they saw reflected in mirrors. An 82-year-old, upper-class woman put it this way: "I am appalled each time I look at my body . . . when I get up in the morning and brush my teeth I look in the mirror and I think, 'Holy Christmas! This is awful!'" A 65-year-old woman who had a middle-class income stated: "Everything kind of sags in spite of all the exercises and all that sort of thing. I must admit I look in the mirror and I really hate that look. I just hate it."

Some women reported that their reflected images, particularly those of their naked bodies in full-length mirrors, were so personally challenging that they avoided them wherever possible. For example, a 65-year-old, upper-class woman conveyed the following: "There are times when I can't look at myself. I won't look at myself in the mirror. I just look so ugly and old. It's the image I have of myself. . . . I don't see any beauty in an older woman's body." For another 73-year-old woman who had a limited income, nakedness in front of either a mirror or her husband of 50 years resulted in feelings of shame and insecurity:

> We've a got mirror on the back of the door. I try to avoid that when I get out of the shower and I'm drying myself. Sometimes I hang my housecoat over it so I can't see it. I'm a disgrace. I should do something about my weight. I'm just ashamed of my body. Sometimes when I get dressed and I have something really nice on that kind of hides it, like a blazer or something, I don't think I look too bad. But I certainly wouldn't let anybody see my body. Not even my husband. Very seldom does he see me naked. . . . I put my nightgown on in the bathroom and I crawl into bed. I go to bed before he does so I'm all covered up when he gets there.

While these sentiments were more common among the older women, very few women suggested that they were comfortable viewing their reflected images in mirrors and photographs, which were perceived to confront them with unpleasant visual cues of their advancing ages and their loss of culturally defined beauty.

Not all women had such strong reactions to their reflected images. Rather than provoking feelings of disgust and anger, some women suggested that mirrors were startling, uncomfortable, and negative reminders that their internal pictures of their bodies and their concomitant felt ages were incongruent with their appearances and their chronological ages. A 72-year-old, middle-class woman put it this way: "Sometimes it's a real surprise when you are walking along the street and you see yourself in the window and you can't believe that's you because you don't feel that old." An 82-year-old woman who had a middle-class income stated: "I'm surprised that it happened—I'm surprised by the amount of deterioration in my appearance." Notably, even the younger women I spoke to expressed similar sentiments, indicating that their relative youthfulness did not render them immune to negativity toward or discomfort with their aging appearances. For example, a 52-year-old middle-class woman had this to say:

I feel the way I've always felt. And then when I look at a picture of myself or I look at myself in the mirror, I don't recognize this person. The person I see in my mind is not actually whom I see in person. . . . I think to myself, "Oh my gosh! How did that happen in a heartbeat?"

In this way, Holstein's (2006) use of Pearlman's concept of "late mid-life astonishment" to explain her own reaction to her reflected image was an apt descriptor of the women's responses to the changes in their physical exteriors relative to their internally perceived identities. The women described experiencing a painful dissonance as they were confronted with the increasing loss of a valued, formerly youthful appearance and the onset of an increasingly disparaged, aging appearance that they struggled to recognize or accept as their own, let alone admire.

Interestingly, an 88-year-old, lower-class woman suggested that not only did she not recognize her body, she did not recognize herself inside the body: "When I look in the mirror, I think somebody's moved in with me. I wonder who the heck it is—it doesn't look like me!" As the women's internal imagery of their bodies collided with the physical realities of growing older and they began to look old and thereby fit the appearances of the "other"—namely, seemingly withered, unattractive older women—the women were confronted with a profoundly unsettling disconnect between their pictures of themselves as youthful, vibrant people and the ageist assumptions they had themselves embraced to their own later life detriment.

## THE LOSING BATTLE OF WEIGHT GAIN

In addition to identifying specific body parts and/or reflected images as particular sources of dismay, many women talked about the changes that had occurred in their overall body shapes and appearances as a result of weight gain in later life. Very few women indicated that they had experienced little or no change in their weight over time, unlike a 71-year-old, middle-class woman who recounted: "I was 128 pounds when I got married and I'm 125 now. I haven't gone up or down over time either. I just stayed the same." While the aforementioned woman noted that she had not worked at maintaining her weight, most of the women who had "stayed the same" had exercised strict discipline over their bodies and their consumption of food. For example, an 81-year-old, middle-class woman had this to say:

> You're damn right I don't let myself gain weight! I put on a kilo, I take it off. Always have acted that way. . . . I say, if I put it on through foolishness—eating, you know—well then I take it off. It used to be if you put on five pounds, you took it off. Now if you put a couple of kilos on you take it off. . . . That's why my body hasn't changed that much. Except the thinning hair—the bald spot up there. And, you know, sagging breasts and gray hair.

In contrast, the majority of women noted that their weight had either fluctuated or gradually increased over time. A small minority of women conveyed feelings of tolerance, good humor, or at least mild satisfaction with their increased body weight. These women made comments similar to those of a 67-year-old, middle-class woman who stated:

> I think I always just sort of took my weight for granted. And now that I'm older and have put on weight, I really think how fortunate I was that I had all those years of, you know, just being slim and not worrying about putting on weight. . . . I'm not really sad about it. I mean, I don't think, "Oh, I've got to get my shape back." I don't really feel that . . . I have put on weight gradually. It just kind of built up and built up and built up. I don't want any more [laughing] but I wouldn't go on a diet.

Although this woman noted that she did not want to become heavier, she laughed easily about her body size and resisted all pressure to alter her weight. However, similar to younger women, the majority of older women expressed dissatisfaction with the fact that they had gained weight over time, as they made comments similar to those of a 76-year-old woman who had a middle-class income:

> I don't like my fat body. Not anymore. . . . I hate to look at a picture. Like yesterday, my daughter brought some down from Christmas. And I think, "Geez, I'm even fatter than I thought I was!" when I look at

the picture. And, of course, I get, "Oh, Mom! You look fine!" from my daughters. But I guess you want to look perfect and you know you don't so you just don't look.

Once again, reflected images in either mirrors or photographs were as much a part of the women's self-recriminations and sense of internal dissonance as bathroom scales. For example, a 51-year-old, middle-class woman reported the following:

> I feel disappointed when I look in the mirror. I think I feel disappointed because when I'm sitting here thinking of myself, I don't think of myself as an overweight person, and then I look in the mirror or I go to the store or whatever and it's like, you know, "Oh gosh!"

Exhibiting the normative discontent (Rodin et al., 1985) expressed by younger women with respect to their weight, the majority of the women indicated that their weight had been a source of lifelong struggle and frustration as they endeavored to achieve and maintain an elusive personal ideal weight. For example, a 58-year-old lesbian, middle-class woman recounted the history of her body weight in this way:

> As a teenager I was not overweight but I had a large frame. I don't know how to describe it. I was chunky. I was never thin, okay. But, as I got older I started the battle of the bulge, and in my 20s and 30s I became really overweight because I went through a period of time, just some hard stuff I was going through, deciding whether I was a lesbian or not a lesbian. So my body changed dramatically over that period of time, in different ways. . . . Later I went through periods of losing weight and gaining it all back. Like in my late 30s and earlier 40s I lost a bunch of weight and then I gained it all back. . . . It wasn't until 2002 that I finally decided that I better get a hold of this cause I was getting really heavy. I was 230 pounds. So, over the last two years I've lost close to 55 pounds and I would like to lose another 20. . . . The weight thing has hounded me throughout my life but it becomes more difficult as you get older because it's more difficult to take it off. . . . I've been on every diet possible.

Using words like "weight problem" or suggesting that they were "battling" or "working hard to lose weight," the women described their body sizes with varying degrees of dismay. Some women noted that their desire to lose weight was, at times, unrealistic as their perceptions of themselves as overweight bodies were skewed. For example, a 65-year-old, middle-class woman asserted: "I was overweight most of my life or, at least, I thought I was. So I've always had that weight thing hanging over my head." Perhaps not surprising given the emphasis on women's weight in contemporary culture, the majority of the women I have interviewed have described having dieted in the past at some time, stated that they were attempting to lose weight at the time of the interview, or recounted that they were constantly vigilant about their food-consumption patterns. The women made comments similar to those of a 63-year-old woman who had a very limited income:

> I'm always on a diet and I'm always conscious of what I'm eating. I think, "Oh my God! Is this going to put a couple of pounds on or could I have another glass of wine?" Or, I think, "Oh! I'm going to get it! I will have problems with weight gain next week!" I'm always trying to lose pounds. I get down there and then something happens and I get depressed and go back three or four pounds and then go down a couple.

The women suggested that the cyclical battle of the weight in which they were engaged culminated in uneasiness and fluctuating contentment with their bodies. A 72-year-old, middle-class woman opined: "I've put on weight and I'm not very happy. I take off a bit and then we go on holidays and it comes back on. So it's an ongoing struggle."

Some of the women indicated that their concern about their weight was augmented by the messages that they received from health care professionals regarding the need to maintain lowered body weights in order to achieve optimal health. For example, a 76-year-old, middle-class woman stated: "Doctors today emphasize weight so much. Years ago, a doctor never even bothered about your weight. But today, the doctors do worry about your weight." Another 67-year-old, middle-class woman relayed the message she had received from her physician about the relationship between her weight and her arthritic hip: "The doctor has been saying . . . 'Just remember that the more weight you put on, the more pressure is on that hip.'"

In addition to the influence of physicians, some women described how they had learned to be concerned about their body weights as well as to diet and discipline their bodies from an early age by watching female significant others such as mothers, sisters, and female friends (Hurd Clarke & Griffin, 2007b). For example, a 56-year-old, middle-class woman recalled:

> My mother was always worried about me gaining weight. . . . My mother was a very buxom woman, so she was always heavy, and she was always on diets and she was always trying to force me on diets . . . and did force me on diets or yell at me. I remember big arguments in the house about that.

In my interviews with women aged 50 to 70, one-quarter of the participants described how their weight had been a focus of concern, if not criticism, for their mothers. They further revealed that concerns about weight and appearance had been passed from one generation to the next as they relayed stories similar to those of a 65-year-old, middle-class woman who reported:

> My grandmother would do things like take my mother after dinner and weigh her every night . . . and my mother was not overweight. She had never been overweight, but there was always this shadow looming. So when I was a kid, I sort of got the same—I wasn't dragged up and weighed but my grandmother was always talking about weight and food.

At the same time, the women's narratives concerning their weights often contained accounts of particular moments in their lives when their weights had begun to be perceived as problematic, either by themselves or by others. A 72-year-old, middle-class woman described the weight issues she had endured since adolescence:

> When I was a teenager, I was very, very fat. That was when I was wearing a size 42 dress. . . . I was a big, fat girl. . . . I've been up and down and up and down a million times. . . . I've always had a tummy but I don't have the big behind that I used to have but I do have fat pads.

Other women stated that there had been a gradual increase in their body weights over time, often following childbirth. Thus, a 72-year-old woman who had an undeclared income stated: "As I got older I put on weight. I put on about ten pounds with each baby." Still other women pinpointed menopause as the point in time at which they had begun to accumulate unwanted weight. For example, a 51-year-old woman who had a middle-class income recounted the following: "I used to be super skinny, and then I went through menopause in, I'd say my late 40s, and after that I put on a few pounds a year, and it just sits on my abdomen." Finally, some women indicated that they had acquired additional weight in later life following the onset of health problems or injuries. Thus, a 77-year-old, middle-class woman stated: "When I broke my hip, I put on 15 pounds sitting about doing nothing and I never took it off."

Not all of the women were dissatisfied with their weights because they felt that they were too heavy. Indeed, it was not uncommon for the women in their late 80s and early 90s to express a desire to gain weight. These women made comments similar to those of a 90-year-old, middle-class woman who opined:

> I wish I weighed more. Yes. If I weighed a little more. I weighed 135 [pounds] at one point. Well, I think that was a healthy weight around my 40s I suppose. But now I think it's more like 125.

Another 90-year-old, middle-class woman suggested that the fact that she was skinny made her "quite hard to look at. . . . You know, with my scrawny neck." These sentiments were shared by younger women who also suggested that it was important for the very elderly not to be overly thin. Despite having maligned her own more curvaceous frame, a 67-year-old, middle-class woman put it this way: "I feel that it's better to have a little bit of weight when you're older because you can be slender when you're younger but then you're scrawny when you're older."

Nevertheless, the most common sentiment among the women was the desire to lose weight. Regardless of when or why their weight had begun to be perceived as being problematic, the majority of women suggested that it had become increasingly difficult to either lose weight or maintain lowered weight levels in later life. For example, a 76-year-old, middle-class woman asserted:

> When you get older, it's not what you eat that puts the weight on. It's, well, first of all, lack of exercise I guess with a lot of people. But I find that it's harder to take weight off when you get older.

The difficulties in losing weight and maintaining lower body weights were often conveyed as a source of profound frustration, as the women made comments similar to those of a 69-year-old, middle-class woman who contended: "I wish I was thinner. I'd love to lose 20 pounds! I would absolutely love to lose 20 pounds! . . . I'm really furious with myself that I can't lose it. You know? I think, 'Why? Why can't I do this?'" In this way, the physical failings of the body hemorrhaged onto and challenged the woman's sense of identity and self-esteem. Indeed, for many women, negative feelings about their weight were exacerbated by the sense of personal culpability. Comparing her sense of responsibility for having gained weight to her lack of personal fault for having developed macular degeneration, a 78-year-old, middle-class woman put it this way:

> I am impatient with my weight gain. That probably bothers me more than my [loss of eyesight] because . . . I had nothing to do with my eyes. I couldn't have prevented that. My weight gain, I have everything to do with it. I think hormonal change certainly is a factor but the rest of it is lack of suitable exercise and probably indulgence. . . . Changes in eyesight and wrinkles—those things you can't do anything about. It's a natural process whereas I don't think my weight gain is a natural process.

These feelings of frustration for weight gain were exacerbated by healthism (Crawford, 1980) or cultural norms pertaining to personal and moral responsibility for maintaining healthy lifestyles, characterized by conformity to weight guidelines and engagement in physical activity. Many older women expressed a sense of guilt and shame for their inability to adhere to societal understandings of healthy living by disciplining and controlling their weights and thereby rendering their bodies attractive as well as healthy. A 73-year-old, middle-class woman stated:

> I think that people feel guilty or ashamed when they're fat because, you know, it's not good for you. It's not healthy. It doesn't look good. But not only that, it's not good for you. And I think they feel sort of—I guess guilty is the best word—because it is something that you can control yourself if you put your mind to it. You can't control the wrinkles. I guess you can control the gray hair. You can color it. And the rest of your appearance, you can modify with makeup depending on what you

wear but there's not much you can do to hide 50 pounds extra if you have it.

In other words, the women's dissatisfaction with their weight was underscored by a sense of moral and appearance failure at not having exercised sufficient control over and discipline of their bodies.

Adherence to healthist norms was further evidenced by the ways in which the women described their motivations to diet (see, for example, Hurd Clarke, 2002b). The women who emphasized the health consequences of having gained weight and the concomitant physical necessities of dieting made statements similar to those of a 65-year-old, middle-class woman:

> My biggest concern about my weight is because of my joints. You know, my knee replacement, which was just in January, and all these things are hard on your body. . . . All the extra weight is hard on your body.

Some of these women were clearly vexed by assumptions that the need to lose weight was the result of cultural beauty ideals and attention to one's appearance rather than adherence to healthy living principles. For example, a 69-year-old, middle-class woman asserted:

> Oh, God! I think everybody is concerned about weight! I think especially as you get older. It sounds odd but it's not just for looks. It's because we get into high cholesterol and heart problems and things like that. And you know that you should be taking your weight down. . . . Like I've put on 20 pounds this last year, which I don't like. I'm not happy about it but not because of what I look like. It's my health. It's not good for me. . . . I worry about my health because, as I say, my cholesterol has gone up again and my doctor nags me a little about it.

In this way, dieting for the sake of appearance was deemed vain and shallow while losing weight for the sake of one's health was perceived to be more socially acceptable, if not required, as well as praiseworthy (Hurd Clarke, 2002b).

However, while the majority of the women argued that health was the legitimate reason for losing weight, they also contended that appearance factors were often the underlying dominant motivating factor in women's choices and behaviors. When asked why people were concerned about their weight, a 76-year-old, middle-class woman replied, "Cause of their looks. How they look. A lot of it is for health reasons but I think it is mostly how they look." Similarly, a 72-year-old woman who had a middle-class income reflected:

> I guess we think that thin, shapely people are beautiful. I suppose that's the real reason. I mean there are a lot of people now who are concerned for their health. They should be if they're not. It really does matter. But I guess it is appearance first; it certainly isn't health first. They wouldn't be doing a lot of other silly things if their health was a real concern.

Therefore, the women's attitudes toward and experiences of losing weight were fraught with conflicting and contentious underlying motivations that they endeavored to negotiate in a way that preserved a positive sense of self in their own eyes and in the perceived views of others.

## GRAY MATTERS: OLDER WOMEN AND THEIR HAIR

There is a growing body of research and theorizing that has explored both the politics of hair and the importance of hair to self-expression (see, for example, Banks, 2000; Furman, 1997; Gerike, 1990; Gimlin, 1996; Koppelman, 1996; Symonds & Holland, 2008; Synnott, 1987; Weitz, 2001, 2005). This research has illuminated the ways that hair is simultaneously a marker of an individual's sense of identity and an indicator of his or her social position and resultant social currency. Specifically, hair is used to express and ascertain a person's age, social class, ethnic affiliation, gender, political inclinations, and sexual preference. While most of the research has explored younger women's experiences of and attitudes toward their hair, there are some studies (Fairhurst, 1998; Furman, 1997; Symonds & Holland, 2008; Winterich, 2007) that have focused on older women. This research reveals that the majority of women perceive gray hair to be a disquieting and unappealing sign of aging that is equated with obsolescence and social devaluation. The researchers collectively found that a woman's decision to dye her hair stemmed from the desire to conceal her chronological age and better approximate the youthful beauty ideal. That said, Winterich (2007) also found that lesbians and women of color were more accepting of gray hair than white, heterosexual, middle-class women and many of the women in Furman's (1997) study liked the appearance of naturally white hair.

In my research during the past 10 years, I have found that similar to weight, gray hair was often identified as one of the markers of old age that was viewed ambivalently by many older women. Using words such as "awful," "unappealing," and "blah," the women frequently suggested that their distaste for gray hair arose from the fact that it appeared "drab" and "nondescript," unlike naturally or unnaturally colored hair. While gray hair is relatively easy to mask, the decision concerning the use or nonuse of hair dye was often an emotional one underscored by complex and ageist meanings attributed to gray hair and aging. Whereas less than half of the women in Study #1 colored their hair, three-quarters of the women in Study #2 and two-thirds of the women in Study #3 dyed their hair. The differences among the women in the three studies may have been the result of sampling whereby more women who dyed their hair participated in the latter two studies as a result of the overall focus of these research projects (non-surgical cosmetic procedures and beauty work). Additionally, the differences in the sample may reflect cohort differences and underlying cultural and historical changes, which distinguish the first study from the second and third studies as well as the older participants from the younger participants in all three studies. For example, Study #1 was conducted prior to the development of anti-aging technologies and marketing strategies, which, in the next chapter, I argue have reflected and capitalized on increasingly negative societal attitudes toward aging appearances and growing pressure to engage in ever more extensive and intrusive beauty work to eliminate even the smallest signs of aging. Similarly, the women's attitudes toward hair dye may have resulted from their socialization and the fact that it was not until the 1930s and 1940s that safer, more effective, and user-friendly hair dyes were developed (Weitz, 2005). Previously associated with sexual wantonness and lower-class status, hair dyes became more socially acceptable in the 1950s as a result of a popular advertising campaign by Clairol (Weitz, 2005). In this way, varying behaviors and attitudes toward the practice of dying one's hair between the studies as well as across the different age groups may have been the result of cohort differences.

Despite the sample differences, there were strong trends in the data that were evident in all three studies. To begin, although they rarely expressed positive sentiments about the look of gray hair, those who did not dye their hair tended to be older. These women contended that the development of gray hair was a natural part of growing older and not something to be viewed with trepidation or repugnance. For example, an 83-year-old, middle-class woman conveyed the following:

> It just seemed a natural part of life. . . . A lot of my friends, as soon as they got their first gray hair they started coloring. . . . But it's a question of time and money. Hair is an expensive sort of thing. So I never did. . . . When I saw my first gray hairs, I thought, "No way am I going to take the trouble to color these."

These women further suggested that getting their hair dyed regularly required more time and effort than they were willing to expend on their appearances. Thus, the women made comments similar to those of an 81-year-old, middle-class woman:

> I think quite a few of my friends have their hair colored. It looks awful when it's growing out. You have to do it regularly. You have to have it done properly. And again it takes time and money. I can't be bothered.

Some of the women argued that their reluctance to engage in this form of beauty work stemmed from the assumption that obviously colored hair looked outlandish, if not disingenuous. For example, a 55-year-old woman who had a very limited income stated: "I guess one reason I don't dye my hair is because it's phoney. . . . Because the real me has got gray hair. Dyeing your hair—it's all trickery." Suggesting that dyed hair culminated in a false as well as sexually promiscuous image, an 86-year-old, upper-class woman put it this way: "It looked too artificial for me so I stopped doing it. I didn't like the look of it when it was colored. It looked too tarty." A few women were particularly scathing of older women who dyed their hair, as they made comments similar to those of a 56-year-old woman who had an undeclared income: "I saw a lady today—she must have been 70 and she had strawberry blonde hair. . . . She looked like Bozo the clown. You know? She would have looked lovely with white hair."

At the same time, a few of the women who did not dye their hair described the sense that their decision not to engage in this form of beauty work put them at greater risk of social exclusion. For example, a 58-year-old, middle-class lesbian woman who described herself as a feminist activist recounted the following incident:

> I went into a restaurant the other day and the waiter turned to me and he says, "Would you like the seniors' menu?" You know, give me a flying break! Now because my hair is going grayer, I've had people say, "Oh, do you qualify yet for the seniors' discount?" . . . I don't like the word "senior" and I don't like feeling segregated.

While she did not esteem the color of her hair and indicated that she missed her formerly darker locks, the woman quoted above indicated that she had decided to "go gray gracefully." She went on to suggest that her disinterest in beauty work such as the use of hair dye stemmed from her earlier socialization. Nevertheless, she described her feelings about her body, aging, and beauty work as an ongoing personal struggle:

> I think it partially comes from how I was raised. My mother used to always say to me, "You shouldn't be vain about yourself." . . . I've taken sociology classes plus I have a long history as a feminist. I was very involved in the women's movement, and I was part of an organization that monitored the media. So I know the image stuff quite well and I know what it does, what advertising does to women. And yet I am not immune at all. It is interesting how it hits me. I'm as vain as the next person around the corner. I'll admit it because this is a research project. Otherwise, I wouldn't admit it. I'm concerned about how I look. . . . I feel quite guilty about the vanity stuff because I have fought so long against it.

While some women tolerated their naturally altered hair color and others found these alterations to be a source of personal turmoil, the women who dyed their hair were definitively negative in their assessments of the appearance of gray hair. A 52-year-old woman who had a middle-class income asserted:

I wouldn't let my hair go gray because I don't like it next to my skin. It makes me look older and I don't like the way I'd look. . . . I personally think it looks terrible on most people. I hate it on myself.

Indeed, the majority of women suggested that gray hair, oldness, and unattractiveness were synonymous. For example, a 65-year-old, middle-class woman maintained: "I look just awful when my hair isn't done . . . just awful—ugly and old." A 67-year-old, middle-class woman put it this way: "Getting gray hair really brings it home that you're getting old." Similarly, a 51-year-old, middle-class woman who had had microdermabrasion in the past in order to look more youthful stated: "I'm sorry but I just don't like gray hair . . . it just doesn't look nice. . . . I think it makes a woman look old—older than she feels probably."

For some women, these feelings about gray hair were long-standing and the product of earlier life experiences. For example, a 51-year-old, lesbian, middle-class woman contended:

Gray to me is bad. I don't like it. It reminds me—my mother was almost always gray or graying my whole life. I spent a lot of time when I was a kid saying to people, "No, she's my mother, not my grandmother." . . . I don't want to be like that. There's nothing that attracts me to gray.

In addition to referring to the existence of less restrictive appearance standards for men, the women often tried to deny their own internalized ageism by suggesting that their disavowal of gray hair had to do with personal taste and individual appearance rather than reflecting a general disparagement of aged-looking bodies. However, by arguing that gray hair was attractive on some individuals, just not on themselves, the women betrayed their own acceptance of ageist appearance discourses, masked in self-deprecating personal descriptions and polite references to others. For example, a 52-year-old, middle-class woman stated: "I don't want gray hair. A lot of people look fantastic with gray hair. I don't think I would. And men look great. Of course men can get away with everything."

Half of the women reported that they had begun dyeing their hair in early adulthood, often, though not exclusively, before the onset of gray hair. When asked why they had first started coloring their hair, some women talked about the importance of adhering to fashion as well as the influence of peers. The women made comments similar to those of an 88-year-old woman who had a very limited income:

> Well, it was the fashion. Everybody did it. . . . You know, it's like buy- ing a new pair of shoes. Why do you wear a certain height of heel or platform? Well, all your friends are doing it so you want to be the same.

Other women contended that changing their hair color was a source of enjoyment and culminated in an attractive look that they preferred over their natural hair color. For example, a 72-year-old woman who had an undeclared income had this to say:

> It has nothing to do with looking younger. That doesn't bother me. I did it for me. I like fooling around. I do my hair—I bleach my own hair. I've done it since I was 16. Just for me. I like the look of it.

Thus, caring for one's hair was perceived to be a pleasurable and feminine activity that the women engaged in for their own sense of personal satisfaction. Still other women indicated that they colored their hair so as to make it easier to style and achieve a desired look. For example, an 84-year-old, middle-class woman asserted: "I have very fine hair and when you dye it you get more body, which is easier to keep. . . . Coloring it has helped, you know, to manage it." Finally, a few women said that they had started going gray at a very early age, prompting them to begin to use hair dye. A 76-year-old, middle-class woman explained: "I've been gray since I was 24. . . . I started coloring my hair then and I've been coloring it ever since." For these women, the initial act of dyeing their hair had to do with the achievement of congruence between their chronological ages and their appearances.

While their reasons for starting to dye their hair at a young age var- ied, most of the women indicated that their motivations for coloring their hair had shifted over time with the onset of gray hair. Similar to the ways in which the women described their dieting practices (see previous chapter), some of the women argued that they colored their hair so as to look more youthful and, therefore, healthy. An 80-year- old, middle-class woman reported:

In the beginning it was just to enhance it more than anything. Then later, of course, it was to not have my age revealed so readily. . . . You want to look as young as you can and as healthy as you can. Also, this is a reason you'll hear many times—that once you started coloring, if you let it grow out you'd look pretty patchy so you just keep on coloring it. But I color mine because I think it looks better

In this way, the women suggested that while they had first colored their hair to conform to fashion trends or to "enhance" their appearances, they had later done so in order to hide the appearance of gray hair and thereby to respond to ageism. Similarly, those women who started using hair dye later in life indicated that they had done so in order to hide their gray hair, which they deemed unattractive and undesirable. For example, a 91-year-old woman who had a very limited income described her experiences in this way: "I was lucky. I didn't start going gray until well into my 70s actually . . . then my hairdresser started lightening it up with a little color, you know, highlights and things. And I've done it ever since." Still other women reported that they had elected to dye their hair for the sake of or because of the influence of others. An 80-year-old, lower-class woman stated:

My friends say, "You look so much better with your hair done—with your hair blonde again." So, oh, well, I have to please my friends. But I feel better, too, with it. And I please my son. When he was here last, he said, "Mother, get your hair blonde again. You don't look like my mother with your hair gray." So I said okay, if it makes him happy.

However, many of the women talked about scenarios in which they might consider not dyeing their hair. To begin, some of the women described shades of gray or white hair that were more attractive than others. For example, a 61-year-old, middle-class woman asserted: "There's all different shades of gray. On some people, it's quite nice looking and other people, it's really, really harsh if it's sort of that black-ish, gray, blue-ish gray color." These women often suggested that if they had what they considered to be an attractive natural color, such as "pure white" or "silvery gray," they might consider letting their hair go gray. For example, a 67-year-old, middle-class woman maintained:

I know some of my friends finally got fed up and let their hair go gray but I haven't been brave enough to do that yet. . . . I have a friend who is 82 this year and she was dark and then her hair went gray and then it went pure white and she looks great. But mine is that iron gray. If it went white, I would let it—I would stop coloring it . . . but I'm not brave enough yet to do that. . . . I can't bear to look at gray hair in the mirror.

While going gray was simultaneously viewed as aesthetically undesirable and an act of perilous heroism, white hair was often identified as the most desirable shade of hair to have in later life in lieu of naturally colored hair. For example, a 76-year-old, middle-class woman stated:

My mother had pure white hair—beautiful white hair! And I wanted that. . . . But I haven't got the head of hair my mother had. I'm a little resentful of that—that I couldn't have had my druthers and had my mother's hair instead of my father's.

Nevertheless, some women foresaw a time in the future or a particular age at which point they would cease coloring their hair. For example, a 51-year-old, middle-class woman had this to say:

I plan to color it until about age 60. I hate to see women who've got an old wrinkly face and dark, colored hair. It just doesn't look right. . . . My mom was gray actually by about age 48 or 50. She let it grow out. . . . I'm hoping for a few more years.

Another 51-year-old, middle-class woman argued:

I'll keep dying my hair probably for another 20 years . . . because an older woman, older than me, with dark hair doesn't look good. . . . I don't want to look like that because that looks too unnatural. The thing I want to keep in mind is looking natural.

Thus, the women made their decisions about dyeing or not dyeing their hair based on their notions of authenticity, definitions of physical attractiveness, and ideas about age-appropriate beauty work. The women's choices were underscored by heteronormative assumptions about feminine beauty, which privileged youthfulness and disparaged aged-looking appearances. While the women did not want to appear old, they also did not want to be obviously engaged in beauty work or seemingly crossing the boundaries of age-appropriate hair color choices. In this way, the women's beauty work actions were emergent as they responded to the physical realities of growing older and the social norms concerning age-specific appearances.

## SHIFTING PRIORITIES AND PRAGMATIC ACCEPTANCE

Despite all the expressed negativity toward their aging appearances, many of the women I interviewed frequently spoke about the need to be accepting of the appearance realities of growing older (Hurd, 2000). Thus, the women often followed their expressions of displeasure with their weight or specific body parts with pragmatic assertions. For example, an 82-year-old, middle-class woman contended: "I'm a realist and these things happen. What the hell do you expect at the age of 82?" Even those women who were strongly invested in their physical appearances tended to share similar views on the need for pragmatic acceptance. A 52-year-old, middle-class woman who used hair dye, makeup, and non-surgical cosmetic procedures to preserve a youthful appearance and was vigilant about maintaining her weight through rigorous exercise and strict monitoring of her food consumption asserted the following:

> About my looks, I'll be just like everybody else. You just get baggier and more wrinkled. I mean that's life. . . . I just think that you have to accept it because it's normal. From a psychological point, you have no choice. So it's silly—it's like being upset about the rain. It's the same thing. It's just like death. I don't want to die. Most people don't. But what are we going to do? It's inevitable. So I think you have to just deal with it.

Although this woman emphasized the need for acceptance of the inevitable bodily changes, her behaviors and obvious investment in her appearance belied her assertions. The juxtaposition of the women's displeasure and frustration with their perceived appearance failures and the sense of a need for resignation often resulted in an uneasy tension. Some women were largely resigned to the fact that they would increasingly deviate from cultural standards of physical attractiveness. For example, a 55-year-old, middle-class woman stated:

> I wish I wasn't putting on the weight that I am as I get older but I guess I have sort of recognized that this is a part of the aging process and the

battle to keep myself slim is not worth the effort. So, therefore, I just think that, you know, I am just going to go with the flow . . . because it would take an inordinate amount of energy for me to try to be slim and I am just not that egotistical. I can't justify that. If I could have a little magic fairy that came along and said, "You know, what would you like to change with your body?" I'd say, "Ah, slimmer would be good." . . . I think that it would be nice to have that 18-year-old body and that 55-year-old brain.

Thus, even as they expressed resignation and appreciation for the wisdom and experience they had acquired over time, the women also bemoaned the loss of their more youthful, sexually desirable, and culturally esteemed bodies. Indeed, many women were clearly discouraged as they made comments similar to those of a 65-year-old, middle-class woman:

The softening of the flesh, as I call it, is inevitable. You can't do anything about that . . . It's frustrating but I've accepted the fact that I'm not going to ever have a 26-inch waistline again. In fact, my stomach is going to hang over a little bit, and the pot is there no matter how hard I work at it. . . . It makes me mad sometimes.

Because beauty and the achievement of beauty standards were largely perceived to be the product of a series of choices, the women's inevitable divergence from attractiveness ideals constituted a moral failure as well as an appearance failure. As will be discussed in the next chapter, the ability of the women to accept the changes in their physical appearances was also being increasingly challenged with the rise of anti-aging medicine and beauty interventions.

At the same time, many of the women reconciled their various feelings about their aging appearances by focusing on their physical abilities and levels of health. Indeed, many of the women tended to follow their expressions of negativity toward their bodies with statements about the triviality of appearance, gratitude for their health, and/or the primacy of health over beauty (Hurd, 2000). A 72-year-old woman who had a middle-class income stated: "Keeping well is the thing you worry about when you're 70. Not so much how it looks as how well it is functioning." A 65-year-old, middle-class woman exclaimed, "I mean I'm 65, I'm not 25. I'm not going to look perfect ever again. . . . I think I'm very lucky to be able to be active." Thus, when asked what they liked most about their bodies, many women made comments similar to those of a 63-year-old woman who had a very limited income:

> I guess my favorite thing is that it still works. It still gets me around. I have friends that are younger than me that are dead. . . . Another friend of mine—it's not going to be long before she's going to be in a wheel-chair. Her whole back is disintegrating with arthritis. . . . So I'm really glad that I come from a family that lives quite long and we're mobile most of those years. . . . I can still play with my grandson—get on the floor and play with him.

In this way, reminiscent of Hochschild's "poor dear hierarchy" (1973, pp. 58–63) and the social comparisons made by participants in Laz's (2003) study, many of the women compared their own bodies and health statuses to those who were much worse off and argued that the negative health experiences of others put their own loss of physical attractiveness into a more meaningful perspective. Invoking internalized ageism and prejudice against disability, the women framed their appearance losses in ways that minimized their own perceived exclusion. That said, other women noted that without the perspective of health and the context of the misfortunes of others, appearance remained important. For example, when asked to rate the importance of appearance on a 10-point scale, a 52-year-old, middle-class woman replied:

> I think it's very important—so appearance on its own, it would be a 10. However, if I were to say, appearance compared to health, well then it would take a much lower priority. Compared to health, I would probably put it at about a six. I would focus more on being healthy than anything.

## SUMMARY AND CONCLUSIONS

In this chapter, I have discussed the complexities of women's feelings about their aging bodies and appearances. The majority of older women in all three studies were displeased with the changes in their appearances that had occurred over time. Specifically, the women expressed discontent with the onset of wrinkles, the development of gray hair, and changes to their body shapes as a result of weight gain and loss of skin elasticity. However, the women's body image negativity did not have an omnipresent or invariable influence on their lives as diverse situations and issues either augmented or diminished their feelings of body dissatisfaction. For example, paralleling Myers and Biocca's (1992) concept of body image as situational and elastic, the women expressed particularly harsh sentiments about their appearances when discussing their naked reflected images where the physical realities of growing older were starkly apparent and ruthlessly scrutinized in the privacy of their bathroom mirrors. In contrast, when speaking about the physical ailments afflicting other older adults, the women tended to downplay the importance of appearance as they emphasized the need for acceptance of the aging process and gratitude for remaining functional abilities. By shifting their emphasis away from the achievement of an idealized appearance and comparing their bodies to their less fortunate peers, the women found meaningful ways to recast their bodies in a more positive light and resist negative aspersions of their personal character and sense of identity. That said, their own positioning of themselves relative to those perceived to be in direr social and health situations reflected their internalized ageism and prejudice against disability.

The women's strongest displeasure was targeted at their weight and specific body parts, including their stomachs, legs, breasts, and arms, although their harsh evaluations were often juxtaposed against their acknowledgment of particular reproductive milestones (such as pregnancy and menopause) associated with increased weight and changes in body shape. Conceding that physical changes were inevitable, the women did not view the gaining of weight to be normative or acceptable. Rather, the women emphasized their personal accountability and moral failure as they framed their perceived need to lose weight in terms of health consequences. The women invoked healthist (Crawford, 1980) norms as they argued that they must control and discipline their bodies in order to be attractive as well as healthy, though the latter was considered to be a more socially acceptable reason for dieting and engaging in other body management activities. The women described how their concerns about their weight and their embracement of healthist norms had been strongly influenced by their interactions with their physicians who endorsed weight control for the sake of optimal aging and health. In this way, the medicalization of weight loss and the omnipresent health promotion messages linking obesity and poor health underscored the women's experiences of growing older and their attitudes toward their bodies.

Given the cultural obsession with youthfulness as an indicator of attractiveness, it is not surprising that the women viewed their physical signs of aging to be undesirable, if not unsightly. The women's acceptance of standards of feminine attractiveness that privileged youthfulness was evidenced by their dislike of the ways in which their bodies betrayed their age as well as in their idealization of their own younger bodies' appearances. Similarly, the women's discomfort with identifying aspects of their bodies that they esteemed or considered more attractive points to the success of their socialization into a culture where women are taught to be normatively discontented (Rodin et al., 1985) with their appearances. The women's difficulty in identifying physical features that they deemed positive and their simultaneous acceptance of the discrepancies and inequities between judgements of older men's and older women's appearances underscored the powerful ways that feminine beauty norms are disempowering and serve to render women docile and insecure (Bordo, 2003). These norms potentially become even more potent in later life when older women increasingly lose their ability to achieve cultural ideals of beauty without drastic beauty work interventions like cosmetic surgery.

Notably, even the self-identified feminists who articulated awareness of the critiques of idealized feminine attractiveness and the power of media imagery were not immune to negative body image. These women conveyed a poignant and deeply personal struggle between their intellectual rejection of misogynist beauty culture, their internalized ageism and sexism, and the social realities of nonconformity. In some ways, these women were positioned in an even more painful conflict than those unfamiliar with or resistant to feminist ideology as their self-awareness, personal values, and daily experiences collided, creating an underlying sense of turmoil. For these women, admitting to concern about their appearances was indicative of vanity and was considered to be evidence of capitulation to sexism.

The women's attitudes toward and responses to gray hair offered important insights into the tensions that women experienced in relation to their appearances and the social realities of growing older. Undoubtedly, the color gray, and specifically gray hair, is one of the most universally recognized markers of old age. As such, gray hair is both a physical attribute and a marker of a woman's social devaluation and exclusion. While the women maintained that gray hair was a normative and inevitable part of growing older, the overarching sentiment was that gray hair was unattractive and undesirable. Consequently, the majority of women dyed their hair, particularly the younger women whose earlier socialization had occurred at a time when hair dyes had become more socially acceptable (Weitz, 2005). Nevertheless, the women rejected the idea that they had internalized ageist discourses as they framed their decisions to alter their hair color as a form of personal pleasure, an act of balancing their felt identities with their appearances, or because they felt that the color gray did not suit their complexions. In this way, none of the women challenged the socially constructed meanings attributed to gray hair and aging bodies. Even those women who did not dye their hair deemed gray hair unappealing. These women asserted that dyeing one's hair was a frivolous and vain response to the aging process, constituted an act of deceit, threatened the integrity of the individual, or simply required too much time and effort to be worth the social dividends of appearing younger.

In many ways, the dilemmas associated with dyeing one's hair are an extension of the growing anti-aging aesthetic movement which has made the options available to women who want to change their appearances more numerous and more affordable. Like non-surgical cosmetic procedures (which will be discussed in the next chapter), hair dyes used at home or in professional salons require much less time and money than more drastic and risky beauty procedures like cosmetic surgeries. In other words, gray hair can be easily, relatively cheaply, and nonintrusively masked in an effort to obfuscate or reject one's social categorization as old. However, the onset of gray hair and the decision to use hair dye seems to be a powerfully emotional and political decision for many women who struggle between acceptance of growing older and internalization of extant beauty ideals that privilege youthfulness. As long as the negative social meanings attributed to gray hair prevail, if not grow in strength, women will face increasing pressure to mask their aging hair so as to be found socially acceptable.

Before concluding this chapter, the shifting of priorities with the development of health issues warrants further comment. Despite all the stated distress and expressions of negativity, the women's feelings about their aging appearances were tempered by the growing realities of health issues. Indeed, the women strongly asserted that physical function was ultimately more important than one's looks even though the fading of a valued appearance was a source of consternation and fostered a sense of loss. Although the women did not challenge the importance of physical attractiveness for women and thereby continued to write and accept their own eventual descent into social devaluation, they argued that the power of extant beauty norms was muted by the more pressing concerns of illness, independence, and dying. In other words, life lessons and the loss of health gradually put appearance concerns into perspective and allowed the women to resist negative evaluations of their identities and social currencies as well as to find positive ways to interpret their aging bodies. That said, while it would be easy and comforting to accept that such a change of heart signalled the emergence of wisdom in later life, it is important to consider that these shifting priorities may have been a rationalization in the face of the women's decreasing ability to successfully engage in beauty culture. In this sense, the apparent throwing off of the burden of beauty ideology was ultimately a call for individuals to resign themselves to exclusion, invisibility, and social devaluation.

## NOTE

1. This topic is pursued more fully in chapter 5.

# 4

⌒↝

# Anti-aging Medicine, Wrinkles, and the Moral Imperative to Modify the Aging Face

"Beauty" is a currency system like the gold standard. Like any economy, it is determined by politics, and in the modern age in the West it is the last, best belief system that keeps male dominance intact. In assigning value to women in a vertical hierarchy according to a culturally imposed physical standard, it is an expression of power relations in which women must un-naturally compete for resources that men have appropriated for themselves. (Wolf, 1991, p. 12)

While gray hair can be easily masked with hair dye, and sagging flesh, stretch marks, and unsightly bulges may be strategically covered with clothing, facial wrinkles have long been a physical marker of aging that is difficult, if not impossible, to hide with over-the-counter beauty products. Previously, cosmetic surgery was the only option available to individuals who were determined to maintain a youthful appearance by ridding their faces of wrinkles, drooping skin, and other evidence of advancing age. However, with the development of anti-aging medicine and beauty interventions, there has been a proliferation of products and services aimed at changing the appearance of the aging face and body. The purpose of this chapter is to specifically examine the social construction of meanings attributed to wrinkles and to explore emergent attitudes toward facial creases and the preservation of a youthful face. I begin by describing the history of non-surgical cosmetic procedures and go on to elucidate the perspectives of physicians who provide these treatments. Next, I explore how the medicalization of wrinkles has influenced older women's attitudes toward their aging faces. Specifically, I analyze how older women perceive their own facial creases using data from qualitative studies conducted before and after the establishment and expansion of non-surgical cosmetic procedures. Highlighting the shifts in women's feelings about wrinkles, the findings from the two studies elucidate the power of the medical community to augment women's insecurity in and the disciplining of their bodies. I conclude by situating older women's perceptions of their appearances within an ageist society that has enthusiastically and uncritically embraced the notion of anti-aging strategies and interventions and the imperative to fight the physical aging process.

## THE RISE OF NON-SURGICAL COSMETIC PROCEDURES

Non-surgical cosmetic procedures include such products as Botox injections, chemical peels, injectable fillers, laser hair removal, microdermabrasion, sclerotherapy, and laser skin treatments. The majority of these procedures are designed to decrease the visibility of wrinkles or add volume to the face in strategic areas, thereby making individuals appear younger. It is difficult to fully ascertain how many of these products and procedures are consumed worldwide on an annual basis. The most comprehensive statistics come from the United States, where according to the American Society for Aesthetic Plastic Surgery (ASAPS) (2010), non-surgical cosmetic procedures accounted for 85 percent of the 9.9 billion cosmetic interventions performed in the United States in 2009. Similar to the trends seen in cosmetic surgery, over 90 percent of the non-surgical cosmetic procedures were purchased by women, with the largest consumer group being White women between the ages of 35 and 50, and the second largest group being White women between the ages of 51 and 64 (ASAPS, 2010).

Although collagen injections and sclerotherapy had been longstanding non-surgical options for individuals seeking to alter their appearances without, or in addition to, surgical intervention, it was the development and marketing of Botox Cosmetic for aesthetic purposes that literally changed the face of aging. Having been used for decades in a variety of capacities (including being used off-label for aesthetic treatments), Botox Cosmetic was first approved in Canada and New Zealand in 2001. Subsequently, the drug was approved in Australia, Taiwan, the United States, Singapore, and Switzerland in 2002. To date, numerous countries allow the use of Botox Cosmetic, although it is sometimes marketed under the brand name of Vistabel (for example, in France and the United Kingdom). A new product, Reloxin, is the latest incarnation of Botox Cosmetic and is currently awaiting authorization for use from the various government agencies such as the Food and Drug Administration in the United States and Health Canada.

The approval of Botox Cosmetic in the early twenty-first century signalled an important change in both aesthetic medicine and the pharmaceutical industry. Suddenly, various alternatives to face-lifts were readily available to demographic groups for whom cosmetic surgery had previously been financially unattainable or undesirable because of the accompanying long recovery process. Relatively noninvasive and financially accessible, Botox has proven to be astonishingly and increasingly lucrative. For example, on their website (http://agn360 .client.shareholder.com/earnings.cfm), Allergan (Earnings Releases, 2008) predicted that their 2008 net sales of Botox Cosmetic would account for between $1,365 million and $1,415 million in profits. According to the ASAPS the top five non-surgical cosmetic interventions performed in 2009 were, in rank order, Botox injections, hyaluronic acid (also known as Hylaform and Restylane) injections, laser hair removal, microdermabrasion, and chemical peels (ASAPS, 2010). Indeed, Botox has been cited as the most popular non-surgical cosmetic procedure in the yearly reports produced by the ASAPS since the drug was approved in 2002. Moreover, the American Society of Plastic Surgeons (ASPS) (2009) reports that in the United States there was a 537 percent increase in the numbers of Botox procedures performed between 2000 and 2008. Even more astounding, ASAPS (2010) reports that between 1997 and 2009, the total number of Botox procedures  performed increased by a whopping 3,825 percent.

Non-surgical cosmetic procedures are marketed as being less expensive, less physically intrusive, and less risky alternatives to surgery. While an individual might end up spending the equivalent of the cost of a face-lift should they undergo repeated non-surgical cosmetic procedures over time, the outlay of cash for each set of procedures is often less onerous and thus seems more financially accessible than surgical options in the short term. It is important to point out that although these products and treatments are typically associated with medical professionals, they are considered to be elective and, therefore, outside the domain of formal health care and, as such, are not covered by the state. Thus, the profits obtained by pharmaceutical companies and physicians come from the disposable income of citizens and not from the government's coffers or private health insurance plans. The relative affordability of non-surgical cosmetic procedures was made particularly evident during the global economic recession. For example, while there were 2.8 million Botox procedures performed in 2007 in the United States, the numbers dipped slightly to 2.4 million in 2008 and held relatively steady at 2.6 million in 2009 (ASAPS, 2010). Thus, during the three-year period there was a decline of 7 percent in the numbers of Botox procedures performed in the United States. In contrast, there was a 22 percent decrease in the number of breast augmentation surgeries (the most popular cosmetic surgery purchased by women) performed during that same three-year period, with no evidence of an end to the downward spiral in the 2009 statistics.

With fat profit margins and a seemingly unquenchable market, Allergan and other pharmaceutical companies are continuing to develop a growing array of synthetic fillers, hyaluronic acids, and other non-surgical cosmetic products, although, to date, nothing has eclipsed the profitability of Botox. Companies have strategically refocused their research, development, and marketing departments from products such as nasal sprays and contact lenses to medical aesthetics, medical dermatology, and obesity interventions. For example, in addition to Botox Cosmetic, Allergan now produces Juvederm (www .allergan.com/treatments/medical_aesthetics/facial_aesthetics.htm), breast implants (www.allergan.com/treatments/medical_aesthetics/ breast_aesthetics.htm), and gastric banding systems (www.allergan .com/treatments/obesity_intervention/index.htm). Positioning itself at the forefront of the fight against aging, the company website states that Allergan is "a global, technology-driven multi-specialty health care company pursuing therapeutic advances to help patients live life to their fullest potential" (www.allergan.com/about/index.htm). The success of the company and the redirection of its focus can be measured in a multitude of ways, including its profit margins; the scope of its markets, which include over 100 countries; and the fact that Forbes.com (2008) reports that Allergan is ranked 1016 in the top 2000 biggest companies (www.forbes.com/2008/04/02/worlds-largest-companies-biz-2000global08-cx_sd_0402global_land.html).

At the same time, the delivery of this type of beauty work has become attractive to a wide range of individuals seeking to cash in on the profits. Thus, the products and procedures are increasingly being administered by nurses, chiropractors, dentists, hair stylists, spa personnel, and others who, especially in the case of injectables, often only need to attend weekend workshops sponsored and organized by the pharmaceutical companies in order to become qualified to provide the treatments. The accompanying certifications are neither monitored nor controlled by the various independent health care professional or medical associations. Although they are not as frequently mentioned in news reports and the majority of the non-surgical cosmetic procedures are delivered in the context of medical clinics, several years ago it was not uncommon to hear about Botox parties that were conducted in the privacy of individuals' homes along the lines of Tupperware parties or book clubs. Certainly, I myself recently went to my dentist office for my regular check-up and cleaning, only to have my dental hygienist proudly announce that my dentist could now give me Botox injections, "although, of course, you don't need them yet." Given that my mouth was full of various dental cleaning equipment at the time of the announcement, I was hard-pressed to voice my objections or indignation, although I managed an unnoticed glare in the direction of the diploma displayed on the wall next to the hydraulic dental chair.

Whether the public was hungry for new ways to defy aging or the pharmaceutical companies created a market with their anxiety-provoking advertisements (which will be further examined in chapter 5), references to and the social acceptance of injectable treatments and other non-surgical cosmetic procedures have infiltrated common parlance and are actively utilized, if not endorsed, by celebrities in the media, particularly those in Western countries. At the same time, non-surgical cosmetic procedures are part of a broader shift in medicine toward anti-aging,[1] formalized through the establishment of the American Academy of Anti-Aging Medicine (A4M) in 1992 (Mykytyn, 2006, 2008). A4M's main objective is "the advancement of technology to detect, prevent, and treat aging related disease and to promote research into methods to retard and optimize the human aging process" (A4M, n.d.). A4M credits Dr. Ronald Klatz with having coined the term *anti-aging* (A4M, n.d.), a concept that was originally defined primarily in terms of longevity and the maintenance of health (Binstock et al., 2006). Indeed, Ronald Klatz has defined the purpose and focus of anti-aging medicine in this way: "We're not about growing old gracefully. We're about never growing old" (Cited in Kuczynski, 1998). Initially, anti-aging medicine was concerned with practices such as diet, exercise, hormone therapies, and supplements designed to optimize the aging process (Fishman et al., 2010; Mykytyn, 2008). More recently, however, the term *anti-aging* has come to be associated with physical appearance in addition to physical health, as one's bodily exterior has increasingly been used as a marker of one's health, morality, and social currency. Everything from lotions and spa treatments to non-surgical procedures are promoted as powerful, if not essential, anti-aging strategies that women, and increasingly men, are required to purchase and apply in order to "defy" and "fight" aging or even "turn back the clock." In this way, appearance has become progressively more important as both the medical community and society at large have increasingly turned to one's body shape, size, and aesthetic appeal as a diagnostic tool for one's health and a signifier of adherence to a socially acceptable and esteemed lifestyle.

## NON-SURGICAL COSMETIC PROCEDURES AND AGING: THE PERSPECTIVES OF PHYSICIANS

With the purpose of investigating how physicians perceived non-surgical cosmetic procedures and their role in anti-aging aesthetic medicine, I conducted interviews with eight physicians (four cosmetic surgeons, two reconstructive surgeons, and two general practitioners) who provided non-surgical cosmetic treatments.[2] All of the study participants were male. When asked why they had moved into the field of non-surgical cosmetic procedures, all of the physicians cited changing patient demands to which they had responded with varying degrees of ambivalence and enthusiasm. Indicating that they had been somewhat reluctant to embrace the new technology and noting that non-surgical cosmetic procedures only constituted between 5 and 15 percent of their practices, the surgeons made comments similar to the following:

> I think plastic surgeons have, like it or not, had to become conversant with these non-surgical modalities because a lot of them work—although a lot of them are completely ineffective—and a lot of them will complement what we can do surgically. And, of course, people are interested in these things and come in and ask and so on. So if you're going to offer comprehensive services to your patients, you have to be conversant with these techniques.

The surgeons further stressed that their preferences laid with the use of their surgical skills and the outcomes that were achievable through surgery:

> I think most surgeons aren't passionately interested in non-surgical cosmetic procedures because we're surgeons. We like to do surgery and that's what we are trained to do. That's where we get our thrills. And certainly most of us are accustomed to bringing about very dramatic changes—the kind of changes that you see when you do surgery. Whereas the improvements that you're able to provide for people using the non-surgical modalities are often very much more subtle and, in some of the modalities in which I don't necessarily believe, so subtle as to be nonexistent.

In contrast, the reconstructive surgeons and general practitioners viewed public demand for non-surgical cosmetic procedures to be an opportunity to engage in more lighthearted medical practice as well as a reprieve from the serious side of working with unhealthy patients:

> It's fun. I enjoy doing it. You're dealing with a different group of people. You're dealing with people who are essentially healthy, who are looking to look better, and people who are generally taking care of themselves.

Thus, aesthetic patients were experienced as less demanding and more pleasant to work with not only because of their superior health, but also because they had successfully embraced and responded to healthist discourses concerning their moral responsibilities to attend to their health and well-being, which was perceived to include their physical appearances.

When asked to articulate why non-surgical cosmetic procedures were increasingly popular, most of the physicians asserted that the allure of the treatments had to do with the shorter recovery times involved:

> We get a lot of requests for the non-surgical stuff. I've been in practice now for 28 years and one of the trends I've seen is there's more reticence to embark on some therapeutic maneuver that has a longer downtime. People want to get something done, and get it done quickly, and be back to work quickly.

When queried about the marketing messages as well as the perception that non-surgical cosmetic procedures were cheaper than surgical interventions, the physicians were quick to point out that the costs of repeated injections or laser treatments "adds up quickly. . . . It's not necessarily a whole lot cheaper, although it's cheaper in terms of usually recovery and downtime, you know, that sort of thing." However, whereas non-surgical cosmetic procedures were considered to be quick-fix alternatives to more invasive surgical procedures such as face-lifts and neck-lifts, the physicians maintained that sooner or later surgery would be the only viable option for those patients who truly wanted to ameliorate their aging appearances. In other words, the physicians contended that their clientele sought out non-surgical cosmetic procedures because they were not yet in the market for more intrusive procedures. With advancing age, increasing facial flaws and other bodily defects would necessitate surgical intervention:

> What we're seeing is both men and women who are coming in earlier and they want more subtle results because they don't have any dramatic changes in their facial aging yet. But they want to kind of stall the advancement of the clock. So we're seeing patients earlier, with more subtle changes, who want to bring themselves back a couple of years. . . . Most of my patients are between 35 and 50 but they go up

to their early 70s . . . late 60s, early 70s is probably the oldest we'll see someone because a lot of these subtle things that we do, the Botox and fillers, at a certain age, if there's enough aging changes, they're not going to be that effective. They need something more pronounced like an eyelid tuck or a face-lift or a neck-lift, or something more pronounced. These fillers, laser resurfacing, hair removal lasers, etcetera, may not be effective with more pronounced aging changes.

The physicians noted that most of the demand for both surgical and non-surgical cosmetic procedures came from women, although their explanations for this phenomenon varied. Acknowledging the pervasiveness of media messages concerning feminine attractiveness and sexuality, some physicians suggested that women's interest in and use of non-surgical cosmetic procedures was simply an extension of their other beauty work efforts:

Women are bombarded—no doubt about it—in magazines. I mean, sex is what drives the planet. Right? And people like to be sexy if they can— a lot of people, anyway. And, you know, part of sex appeal is wearing the right clothes, looking the right way. It's just a reality whether we like to believe it or not. That's why we exist. So I think there'll be social pressures and probably more and more people who will feel a little bit more pressured into having these procedures done. But I don't think that's any different than fashion and other kinds of things. . . . I mean, women in particular have always been trying to look better whether it's make-up or hair-dos or whatever the heck it is.

Other physicians referred to the gender relations underlying women's greater attention to their appearances, as they made comments such as: "There's a lot more societal pressure on women to look good than there is for men. Women get old, men just age." One physician illuminated the oppressive nature of the disciplining of female appearances by juxtaposing women's experiences with those of his own:

As a male, I don't feel a lot of pressure about my appearance. So it's not like I'm looking in the mirror every day going, "Oh jeez, that wrinkle's really gonna impair my ability to work or have a social life," or whatever. So, you know, I'm sure I looked better when I had some Botox in but I don't really care. So, you know, I sympathize for my patients. . . . I feel as though women have a very difficult, sort of, pressure on them to look good physically. And that their physical appearance is extremely important. And as a result, their physical appearance is very important for their self-esteem. And I think they're very motivated to look their best. I think that's unfortunate. I don't know why that is. You know, is it a genetic issue? Is it some sort of hard wiring that we have as humans? Does it have to do with procreation? Who knows? I don't know why there's this pressure on women. But I don't feel it as a man.

Despite his awareness of greater societal pressures confronting women, this physician was unsure of the origins of these inequities. He, like some of his other colleagues, suggested that the discrepancies related to women's and men's appearance requirements had to do with biological differences rather than to sexist beauty discourses. One physician put it this way: "Men, uh, their skin is thicker than women's. And so when women age, they're going to look older because their skin is thinner. And so maybe that's a reason why more women come in for these procedures." Thus, even though the physicians expressed awareness of the greater pressure imposed on women with respect to the need to do beauty work and thereby do gender, they attributed this pressure to innate biological differences, which served to obscure their own role in women's oppression.

While the physicians were careful to not disparage the appearance of wrinkles or to directly suggest that aged faces were unappealing, many of the physicians' comments were buttressed by ageist discourses. For example, the physicians perceived their professional purpose to be as follows: "What we want to do is make you look good for your age." This seemingly innocuous statement belied the underlying message that the individual's ability to "look good" was limited by her age and her willingness to engage in aesthetic medicine. According to this perspective, the role of aesthetic medicine was to compensate for nature and for the ravages of time by "rejuvenating" and "refreshing" the body, thereby making it look younger. These findings are similar to those of Fishman et al. (2010) who reported that the anti-aging practitioners in their study perceived their role to be the collaborative optimization of the health of their patients. Stressing the importance of achieving an optimal appearance, the physicians I spoke with often suggested that fears about getting older were normative and logical responses as later life was positioned as a socially devalued and physically diminished part of the life course that should be "fought" against:

> Most people aren't reveling in the thought of getting older. The aesthetic patients never come to me and say, "Wow, this is great! In another five years, I'm going to be 60. I can't wait!" I mean, it's better than the other option, but you know, they all say, "I wish I could stop right here. I'd like the experience I have but I just don't like the deterioration in my muscle strength and my motor coordination and the aesthetic appearance that happens with aging. So, I do want to fight some of that."

The physicians noted that they personally shared this view, and many described personal regimens for fighting aging and resisting looking aged that they themselves followed religiously: "It's a very simple protocol: Exercise, sun protection, no smoking, half-decent nutrition, dressing your age but not more, and . . . then the aesthetic stuff just to fight the external appearance of gradually growing older." The physicians further noted that the purpose of these strategies was to maintain their youthfulness and thereby retain their appearance capital. The physicians accounted for the importance of youthfulness in this way: "I think that relates to this emphasis on youth. Youth rule the world . . . and youth is everywhere." Another physician put it this way: "In today's society youth is worshipped and so people just don't feel comfortable getting old." Accordingly, looking aged was considered to be a deviant state and an unnecessary source of anguish and "suffering" that could easily be addressed with a myriad of technological advancements: "I think a whole bunch of things have culminated to change aging. Viagra, Human Growth Hormone, the Anti-Aging Academy, non-surgical techniques. All of those have culminated in this thing that you don't need to suffer aging." In other words, whereas aging once had been a hopeless process that resulted in one's social and physical ruin, the physicians argued that the combination of biomedicine and aesthetic medicine afforded individuals an avenue for deliverance.

However, several of the physicians were strongly opposed to the assumption that their clients sought out non-surgical and surgical procedures merely to look younger, which was considered to be a vain and simplistic assessment of their motivations:

> You have this idea that everybody's trying to look young, they're try-ing to beat the clock, they can't age gracefully, and so on and so forth. That's not been my experience. My experience has been that they don't like some of the things that come along with the aging face being on a planet that has gravity. But my patients are not trying to fool the rest of the world into thinking, "Gosh, they're 25," when really they're 37. I mean, you read the popular press and it sounds like that's all they want to do. But that's not been my experience with the last 40,000 patients I've taken care of. Patients have specific things they don't like. . . . You might say these things make them look older, but if you talk to them and say, "Well, is your motivation that you want to look younger?" They'll say, "No, I just, I don't like this. I don't like the haggard look."

Rather than responding to internalized ageism and socially con-structed definitions of idealized beauty that deemed aged appear-ances to be abhorrent, the clients were seen as rational actors and "savvy cultural negotiators" (Gimlin, 2000, p. 96) seeking to justifiably ameliorate specific bodily flaws that were indeed unattractive.

Another way that ageism pervaded the physicians' discourses was in the construction of a dichotomy between the privileged status of feeling and being perceived as young and the devalued state of looking and being old. Specifically, many physicians stated that the reasons their patients used non-surgical cosmetic procedures was to achieve congruence between their felt identities as non-old individu-als and their appearances:

> The patients I see—the reason they are having these done is because they really aren't feeling their age. They're active . . . and they don't feel like they are getting old the way our parents got old. I think before people went, "Okay, I'm in this phase of my life, this is how I should look, this is how I should act." And everyone did that, so that was the norm. Now, they're in better shape. They are in pretty high profile jobs. There's still income coming in. They're not really thinking about slowing down to any great degree. They're going to go for a lot longer period of time. And they start to see some changes and they say, "Hey! Maybe I'm 52, but damned if I'm going to look like 52. Because I don't feel like 52 and I don't want to look 52—like my mother or father when they were 52.

I'm going to do everything I can to prevent myself from heading along that slope." . . . Fifty-year-olds now, whether they're faking it or not, still think they are in their 30s. . . . People are fighting getting old. And I think another way of fighting this getting old is aesthetically.

Thus, to feel and to look one's chronological age as an older adult was to risk being associated with negative stereotypes of later life and thereby considered to have become socially obsolete and unengaged. In contrast, the physicians argued that altering one's appearance through engagement in aesthetic medicine could actually alter one's age and improve one's health:

> LAURA HURD CLARKE: I'm intrigued by the idea that people don't want to "get old." Obviously making their faces look young isn't preventing them from getting old. It's kind of a strange tension.

> PARTICIPANT: No, not really. No, because when people look younger, they tend to feel younger. And feeling younger is good. Good for your health, yeah. You start to feel old, you get old.

Refuting the critique that looking old and being old were separate, if not disparate, issues, the physicians contended that one's appearance and one's felt identity were the true markers of one's age rather than one's chronological age.

At the same time, the physicians identified two main groups among those who resisted "getting old" by using aesthetic medicine to make their appearances mirror their inner ages. Suggesting that they "just don't want to get old" and that they "are more aggressive in seeking these treatments," some physicians identified baby boomers as a cohort that was particularly concerned about achieving and maintaining continuities between their felt identities and appearances:

> They have the teaser that there's going to be some breakthroughs in longevity and anti-aging and yet they're still seeing things deteriorate externally at the same pace as their parents did. . . . They want to sort of pair up their appearance with that internal sense. And I think there's an imbalance between what people see when they look in the mirror and how they feel inside, very often, that they're looking to bring back into harmony.

Similarly, the physicians argued that their female patients often wanted to use non-surgical cosmetic procedures in order to achieve congruity between their appearances and their sense of themselves as healthy and youthful individuals:

> There's really an increasing group of women that want to look natural and they want to be healthy and they want their looks to reflect that. So it's not just a superficial, you know, "Fix me up, give me a little Botox and fillers and some laser stuff." They feel good. They feel young. And they want their face to look—to reflect that. Even women in their 60s. I mean, some of them are very attractive-looking women and they don't consider themselves to be older women at all. Whereas, my parents, when they were 60, I guess they were old folks. But now 60 is the new 40. . . . It makes the women feel better about aging. I think it makes them realize that they don't have to necessarily look haggard. Tired. They can brighten their face up a little bit. . . . But, you know, aging is going to happen anyway and I think people's job is really to remain as healthy as they can by doing all the very, very basic things. . . . I think these non-surgical cosmetic procedures can give people quite a nice lift.

Rather than being a "superficial" act or the product of gender and age relations, the use of non-surgical cosmetic procedures to ameliorate one's aging and, therefore, "haggard," undesirable, and devalued appearance was presented as a health intervention with both appearance and psychological dividends. Non-surgical cosmetic procedures were positioned as a strategy for bringing harmony and congruence between an individual's identity and their level of health, social engagement, felt age, and possession of the most valued of social commodities, namely youthfulness.

## INTERVIEWS WITH WOMEN BEFORE THE RISE OF NON-SURGICAL COSMETIC PROCEDURES

While the statistics regarding the use of non-surgical cosmetic procedures are truly staggering and the view from inside the field is that aesthetic medicine will only continue to grow, there has been limited examination of the impact of this new form of beauty work on women and their experiences of growing older. The growing emphasis on looking youthful and the copious beauty strategies and interventions with which women are expected to avail themselves have culminated in increasingly unattainable appearance demands for women in later life. These beauty work expectations are often costly, increasingly time consuming, and difficult to navigate given the physical changes that occur with time and the elusiveness of the beauty ideal.

To elucidate these challenges, it is helpful to investigate how older women perceive the impact of aging on their facial appearances and how these perceptions mirror developments in technology and changes in aesthetic medicine. To begin, I draw upon data from interviews with women (Study #1) that were conducted in 1998 before non-surgical cosmetic procedures took off. While they were not specifically asked about their opinions regarding their facial creases, all of the 22 women in the study (aged 61 to 92) had strong opinions about their wrinkles, which repeatedly emerged in the course of our conversations. Evidencing the internalization of ageist conceptualizations of physical attractiveness, half of the women contended that wrinkles were unappealing and undesirable, as they made comments similar to those of an 82-year-old, middle-class woman:

> I think it bothers everybody. You look in the mirror and you think, "Oh my God! Look at that face." You know? Let's face it. I'm looking at your beautiful skin and your lovely complexion and I think, "Isn't that nice?" . . . You can have my wrinkles any time you want. I'd gladly give them to you. . . . When you see people that have lived a long time—like in their late 90s—or a picture of them or something, it's kind of sad that they have all—that we all get wrinkles. It'd be nice if that could be eliminated.

The above expression of the desire to eliminate wrinkles is particularly important, if not prescient, given that Botox Cosmetic had not yet been approved as an aesthetic treatment. For many women, the onset of wrinkles and the concomitant loss of a youthful looking face was a source of sadness that they tried to mitigate with humor and references to social truisms refuting the importance of appearance. For example, a 67-year-old, middle-class woman had this to say:

> I notice a particular change between the ages of 60 and 67. Each year when I look in the mirror, I think, "Oh, there's another wrinkle in my face. Where did that come from?" . . . It's hard to look at yourself in

the mirror. I remember my mother saying, "Oh, well, as long as you're clean and presentable." I think of that expression every time I look in the mirror. I say, "Well, I've had a shower and I'm clean and presentable, anyway. I may not look glamorous but there I am." And who was it that said when we were younger we all wanted to look like Elizabeth Taylor and now, by God, we do?

The women frequently expressed a profound sense of shock and dismay at the increased wrinkling in their faces that had occurred over time and asserted that wrinkles made older adults look "crabby," "grouchy," "withered," "miserable," "ugly," and "unattractive." Thus, wrinkles simultaneously evoked negative emotions and were assumed to exemplify negative emotional states, which were, in turn, equated with feeling and being old. The women who disliked their wrinkles also indicated that they were open to considering cosmetic surgery and/or supportive of others who turned to surgical interventions such as face-lifts to remove the offending facial creases. However, many of the women, irrespective of their social class, cited financial resources as the underlying factor that had delimited their decision to not go under the knife. For example, an 80-year-old, lower-class woman had this to say: "I think cosmetic surgery is marvellous for some people. I would have it done if I found that I was getting too wrinkled and if I had the money. I would get the whole face lifted." Similar to the physicians that I interviewed, the women considered beauty work to be a form of health promotion. The women further maintained that attending to one's physical attractiveness and do-ing things to look as young as possible were requirements for social participation and inclusion. For example, a 67-year-old, middle-class woman stated:

I'm not opposed to cosmetic surgery. I don't feel, "Don't ever do that. You shouldn't. You're vain." . . . I think if it's done for the right reasons, it's fine. And I could see people wanting to do it. . . . I just see it as a natural progression. People are living longer. They're maintaining their body strength. They're interested in things around them. They want to participate. And I just think it'll probably become sort of like taking vita-mins. You know? You take vitamins to maintain your health. You have a nip and tuck here to maintain your face.

Therefore, the women viewed cosmetic surgery as an acceptable, if not a moral, response to increasing longevity and the appearance deficits associated with growing older. In this way, the women expressed many of the sentiments commonly found in anti aging marketing, which will be examined further in the next chapter. Specifically, the women suggested that appearance interventions were the logical and positive extension of healthy living ideologies and that choosing to not fight or remove facial wrinkles with any number of the available products and services constituted a moral violation.

In contrast, the other half of the women viewed wrinkles as badges of honor that they had earned over time and that they would not consider having altered. That said, these women were also not pleased with the development of facial creases, as expressed by a 69-year-old, middle-class woman who contended:

> I'm not thrilled to pieces that I've got wrinkles and bulges here and there but that's part of living. I am not into worrying about things like that. . . . I've earned all my wrinkles. I've earned everything. I want to be just the way I am. I'm fine. . . . I would never go out and get face-lifts and body tucks and all that crap. I think that's stupid.

Despite their stated displeasure with their facial creases, the women suggested that acceptance of the realities of growing older and the viewing of the physical changes as emblematic of morality was important. A 76-year-old, middle-class woman stated: "There was a movie star who said every wrinkle was a sign of her life—that her wrinkles were her life on her face. If you don't have wrinkles, you haven't had much of a life." Similarly, an 82-year-old, middle-class woman had this to say:

> Wrinkles—well, that's part of life. I have to accept that. . . . Sure, I'd like to have skin like you. I'd love it. But it doesn't really matter. . . . You associate with a group of people. As you age, they age. So you don't really notice.

Consequently, the women's assertions that individuals need to accept the physical realities of aging were juxtaposed against their own

awareness and internalization of the societal disparagement of aging
and aged appearances.

In addition to advocating the need for acceptance, the women
who offered more positive views of their wrinkles contextualized
their experiences in relation to health and illness. Specifically, many
of these women also asserted that compared to the potential loss of
health and physical independence, the onset of wrinkles was of little
consequence. For example, an 83-year-old, middle-class woman maintained: "Wrinkles. Well, why worry about that? I mean, that's trivial,
isn't it? As long as we can get around, that's what is important."
Whereas the women were clearly aware that their aging appearances
excluded them from societal definitions of beauty and sexual attractiveness, they were also cognizant of the fact that the complete loss of
functionality would lead to total social exclusion. Thus, ageism was
experienced as a continuum whereby individuals were first labelled
as decreasingly attractive and then ultimately denied access to social
participation by virtue of the limitations of their bodies, societal attitudes regarding frailty and disability, and the built environment.

Among those who advocated acceptance of wrinkles, some of the
women expressed sympathy toward others' decisions to undergo surgery even as they indicated that they themselves would never assent
to medical intervention for their appearances. For example, a 73-year-
old woman who had a limited income stated:

> I know I've got all kinds of wrinkles but they don't bother me. I say I
> earned every one of them. . . . I shouldn't make that assumption of most
> women but I would say a lot of women are bothered by their wrinkles.
> Like, how many people have face-lifts and things like that? But I would
> never think of doing anything like that. I mean, my wrinkles are me.
> . . . It's just part of growing old, as far as I'm concerned. I mean, like, a
> lot of people grow old and they don't get a lot of wrinkles, but I always
> say I earned mine from smiling or—I don't know. So, it doesn't bother
> me. Not very often I look in the mirror and think, "Oh, my gosh. Look
> at those wrinkles!"

Other women were strongly opposed to surgical interventions and
vociferous in their criticisms of the industry, society, and others who
pursued such options. An 86-year-old, middle-class woman asserted:

> Cosmetic surgery is just a bunch of shit. Anybody that goes into that is really, really sad. It's sad that they have to do that to change themselves. It's sad that we've come to that. It really is sad. . . . I think it's absolutely silly. It's not worth it. What are you doing mutilating yourself? . . . Oh, God. I think it's ridiculous.

Indeed, these women tended to view those who either expressed dissatisfaction with their wrinkles and/or who were considering or had had cosmetic surgery to be "terribly vain," "sick," and "superficial."

## INTERVIEWS WITH WOMEN AFTER THE DEVELOPMENT OF NON-SURGICAL COSMETIC PROCEDURES

Conducted in 2005, Study #2 entailed interviews with 21 women who had used a range of non-surgical cosmetic procedures and 23 women who had not used any of these types of beauty interventions. The women were all aged 50 to 70 and had an average age of 58 years. Of these 44 women, only three indicated that they liked their facial creases as they made comments similar to those of a 55-year-old, lesbian, middle-class woman: "I love an aging face. . . . My partner says to me, 'Oh! You're getting lines.' But I like my lines. There's nothing wrong with my lines." Four other women expressed sentiments similar to those found in Study #1 participants as they maintained that they were not distressed by the onset of their wrinkles, mainly because they did not pay attention to them. Notably, one of these four women had had laser resurfacing and another was using Restylane, Botox, and Dermalive to decrease her facial creases, which seemed to contradict their stated resignation toward having wrinkles. Echoing the sentiments of the physicians who argued that individuals turned to non-surgical cosmetic procedures in order to create synergy between their appearances and their perception of themselves as internally youthful irrespective of their chronological years, the latter woman had this to say:

> To me, having little wrinkle lines is not a big deal. I don't want to look young. I'm just not ready to look old yet. I don't want to look 30 or 20. I just want to look a bit younger. . . . I felt good after I had the Botox and

the lips done cause I felt I looked—I saw myself as looking younger. I could actually see that I didn't have the frown anymore. (age 52, and with a middle-class income)

The remaining two women made comments similar to those of a 56-year-old, middle-class woman who had not used any non-surgical cosmetic procedures:

I'm very comfortable where I am right now. Using Botox or getting a face-lift just doesn't appeal to me. I feel that I can spend money on better things. I've got enough to worry about without worrying about if I've got one more wrinkle or one more sag.

The truism about "earning one's wrinkles" was noticeably absent from the women's narratives, and only two women out of the entire sample suggested that "a wrinkled face is a face that's been through some stuff" (a 64-year-old, upper-class woman). In fact, some women openly derided the expression, as conveyed by a 65-year-old, middle-class woman:

It always bugs me when people say, "I earned every damn one of these wrinkles and I'm proud of it." I think, "You're protesting a bit too much!" And I think, "Oh give me a break!" I mean, if you're not aware of it then you wouldn't even be mentioning it. It seems like a bit of a pose: "Well, I'm getting old, and I'm really happy about that." I suppose if you're going to consider the alternative, yes, you could be happy about it. But I don't think anybody's really overjoyed that things are beginning to break down or slow down. I mean, come on!

true

Refuting the assertion that the onset of wrinkles was an acceptable, if not positive, development, many of the women argued that facial creases were not only unattractive, but they also signified internal physical decline that was assumed to be an inevitable outcome of aging. Two-thirds of the women described the onset of wrinkles and the appearance of facial creases negatively. A few women, who tended to be younger and, therefore, had fewer facial creases, expressed mild irritation with their wrinkles but qualified their comments by saying that they did not invest a lot of time worrying about the changes that were occurring in their appearances:

I don't have a lot of wrinkles. I guess I think about them when I have to deal with them—like in the morning when I'm washing my face and I'm looking in the mirror. I don't sit around and obsess about them but I do notice them. . . . I'm not really thrilled with the beginning of a lack of firmness in my face. (age 56, middle-class income)

Some women were also pragmatic, as they counterbalanced their expressions of negativity with assertions that becoming wrinkled was a normative part of growing older. For example, a 52-year-old, middle-class woman stated:

As for the wrinkles, I would say that I'm not thrilled with them. But, it's not cancer. It's all relative. . . . I'll be like everybody else—you get baggier and more wrinkled the older you get. I mean, that's life.

However, some of the women were intensely displeased about their bodily wrinkles, as evidenced by the comments of a 55-year-old, lower-class woman who asserted: "As for wrinkles, I hate them all, I don't think a person looks good with lines." These comments were particularly, though not exclusively, common among those who were older. For example, a 65-year-old, middle-class woman put it this way:

It's very difficult to see the wrinkles appearing and the skin losing its elasticity. . . . I have considered the same things that my sister has considered—getting rid of these wrinkles, and the face-lifts and all that. Whether I'll ever do it or not, I don't know, but certainly I've considered it. I probably won't do it, but that doesn't stop me from thinking about doing it every time I look in the mirror and I see these wrinkles. . . . We know we're going to get wrinkles but . . . if we think about it, it can be too painful. So I know with myself, I don't go there, it's too incomprehensible. But I'm not very accepting of death, so I'm not very accepting of wrinkles either.

Referencing the contemporary blurring of health and appearance, these women took a profoundly dim view of facial creases as they argued that the onset of wrinkles signified internal aging, physical deterioration, and impending death.

At the same time, the women tended to view certain types of facial wrinkles more negatively than others. Corresponding with the wrinkles targeted by non-surgical cosmetic procedures such as Botox injections and injectable fillers, the women pinpointed creases in their brows or around their mouths as being particularly abhorrent. For example, a 59-year-old, middle-class woman who used Botox and collagen injections described her wrinkles in this way:

> I don't have a problem with the lines on my face—I consider them to be laughter and character lines. But I don't like these lines below my mouth because they make my mouth look sad and I don't like the lines in my brow because they make me look cross. If I hold my face up, the sides, and take away this double chin, I'm taking 10 years off myself.

Indeed, the women suggested that the unwanted wrinkles made their faces look "angry," "crabby," "cross," "droopy," "grouchy," "hatchet faced," and "mad," and, therefore, old and unattractive. In contrast, the other facial creases, particularly those around the eyes, were described in less emotion-laden and pejorative terms as "character lines" and "crow's feet." ? sounds pejorative

Despite their strong tendency to view their wrinkles disparagingly, particularly those associated with negative emotions and concomitantly with oldness, three-quarters of the women were opposed to cosmetic surgery, which they tended to describe as "drastic," "extreme," "excessive," and "risky." The women made comments similar to those of a 71-year-old, middle-class woman who had employed non-surgical cosmetic procedures (microdermabrasion) in the past: "I mean wild horses wouldn't drag me into cosmetic surgery. You know, I'm not perfect in any way but you couldn't get me near that. You couldn't pay me enough. I'm not into that." Other women emphasized the danger of "going under the knife" as they articulated sentiments similar to those of a 51-year-old, middle-class woman who had used non-surgical cosmetic procedures, specifically Thermage:

> I won't have surgery. I won't go to the extreme. I'm not courageous enough to be put under a general anaesthetic for body altering stuff. I don't want anything under a local either. I won't even have laser surgery for my eyes. I'm so scared of it. I'm very scared of those things.

Still other women expressed ambivalence as they acknowledged that in the future they might consider having cosmetic surgery, specifically face-lifts. A 53-year-old, middle-class woman who had not yet tried non-surgical or surgical cosmetic procedures stated:

> I won't rule it out forever. In another ten years, I don't know, if I have the money that I absolutely don't know what to do with and the lines become disturbing to me or whatever—the lines under my eyes—maybe I would do something.

While their comments suggested that they probably would not pursue cosmetic surgery, they were not willing to completely preclude the possibility. In this way, the women's underlying anxiety over what the ravages of time would do to their faces rather than the desire to be more attractive (see also Henderson-King & Henderson-King, 2005) made surgery a future option that they might be open to considering. Interestingly, of the 44 women in the study, one had had an abdominoplasty and liposuction, two had had breast reductions, one had had a breast augmentation, and one had undergone breast reconstruction following a mastectomy. Only one of the women who had previously had surgery was open to considering future cosmetic surgical procedures because of her satisfaction with the procedures she had done in the past:

> There's a lady that works at the bank and when I see her, I can see on her face that she is embarrassed by her appearance. Where I feel myself, I walk into a place and I have so much confidence, I can just face anything. I don't have to hide anything. I don't have to be embarrassed because I have had certain things done and I'm happy with the results. (age 53, middle-class income, had had laser hair removal, abdominoplasty, and liposuction)

In contrast, the other women made it very clear that they would not even entertain the idea of having additional surgery to alter their appearances.

Although the majority of the women were against having cosmetic surgery, their attitudes toward non-surgical cosmetic procedures were more varied and frequently more positive. To begin, of the 21 women who had had non-surgical cosmetic procedures in the past, 16 women were very satisfied with the results, three women were moderately satisfied, and two women were extremely dissatisfied as a result of complications that had ensued from the treatments. The women who were pleased with the transformations in their appearances as a result of the non-surgical cosmetic procedures tended to comment on how the beauty interventions had made them look younger, which in turn, had enhanced their self-confidence and contributed to an improved sense of well-being. A 65-year-old, middle-class woman who had had Botox and Restylane injections had this to say: "I just think it's made . . . my face look much younger . . . [and] I feel much better about myself." Some women also described their pleasure with the effects of the non-surgical cosmetic procedures by referring to the perceived health and appearance benefits of the beauty interventions. For example, a 60-year-old, middle-class woman described how she began to use Botox, Restylane, and Perlane injections in order to look healthier and, therefore, younger following a myocardial infarction:

> I was feeling so down that summer and I was feeling so old and . . . look-
> ing old. . . . I phoned the doctor up and I think it was about three weeks
> after my heart attack actually and I said, "Okay, do something. I need
> something to pick me up. . . . I shouldn't be here. I've just had a heart at-
> tack but help me. Do something. Make me feel better." So she did the Bo-
> tox on the brow and then she put the Restylane in the lip, you know the
> Perlane and stuff like that . . . and oh! It just—I just, "Wow, this is great!"
> . . . I felt so young. . . . I said, "I look so much softer. I look friendlier."
> And I just really liked the way it looked. . . . For me, it was very uplifting.

Having internalized the societal linkage of health, youthfulness, and appearance, this woman contended that the use of non-surgical cosmetic procedures were integral to her self-esteem, well-being, and recovery process. Although she articulated awareness that such interventions might have been contraindicated by her health problems, she maintained that the psychological and appearance benefits were worth the risk. Not surprisingly, the women who had had positive experiences with non-surgical cosmetic procedures were more than willing to consider additional procedures in the future, particularly as new and possibly better beauty interventions became available. The women who expressed dissatisfaction with the results of their previous non-surgical cosmetic treatments were also willing to consider future procedures, but only once they were convinced of the safety and the unlikelihood of incurring any negative health side effects. For these women, the possibility of achieving a more youthful and desirable appearance outweighed the potential risks. Like the women who were satisfied with the procedures they had previously received, these women accepted the privileging of youthfulness in Western society and emphasized the self-esteem and appearance dividends of appearing younger.

In contrast, the women who had not tried any non-surgical cosmetic procedures were roughly divided in half with respect to their openness to purchasing any procedures in the future. Most of the women who suggested that they might consider trying one or more non-surgical cosmetic procedures had specific treatments that were of interest to them. For example, a 56-year-old, middle-class woman stated the following: "I would consider laser resurfacing for the fine lines around my mouth." A 55-year-old, lower-class woman asserted: "I would go for the Botox or the laser therapy or the injectable fillers. I am getting some lines on my face now and I would probably do some of those things if it was possible financially and if it doesn't hurt you." As well as the onset of fine lines, some women suggested that they might try procedures that would reduce facial sagging. For example, a 51-year-old, middle-class woman had this to say:

> I probably would consider Botox and the other stuff because sometimes I look in the mirror and the wrinkles themselves don't bother me, what bothers me is the stuff down here, the jowls. Because I think . . . my face looks unhappy or angry sometimes.

Whereas the women quoted above were noncommittal as to whether or not these expressions of interest would move beyond contemplation to action, their openness to at least some non-surgical cosmetic procedures was markedly different from sentiments expressed by 13 of the women who had never had any non-surgical cosmetic procedures. Some of these latter women expressed strong concerns about the safety of any or all non-surgical cosmetic procedures as they made statements similar to those of a 64-year-old, middle-class woman: "My approach is that I'd like to look as good as I can but I don't want any invasive or potentially harmful procedures. Face-lifts, Botox, even the skin peels and stuff scare me!" Several women conveyed vehement opposition on moral grounds, as expressed by a 60-year-old, lesbian, middle-class woman:

> To me, it's violence against your body to do things like that. . . . I don't think it's okay. Of course, I believe that women have a right to choose what they want to do with their bodies and if they want to do violence to their bodies, to me they need help. . . . So I think that it's wrong. . . . I think it's sad that women feel they have to do that.

At the same time, Botox and injectable fillers were the target of particular criticisms among half of the women who had had procedures and more than half of the women who had not previously had any non-surgical cosmetic procedures. While they were interested in and supportive of surface treatments such as microdermabrasion, laser skin treatments, and chemical peels, they felt that any treatments that transgressed the body's surface were unacceptable. These women used words like "risky," "unhealthy," "crazy," "radical," "invasive," and "extreme" to describe Botox injections and injectable fillers. A 62-year-old, lower-class woman had this to say:

> I just think injecting stuff into your body is crazy. Who knows down the road what that is going to do? . . . What is going to happen to your mind or your body because of this stuff? I would never consider anything like that. . . . If a friend told me they were going to do this, I'd say "Why would you do that? Have you thought down the road of what is going to happen?" . . . Like your lips might crack and blow up! . . . If I could, I would get that microdermabrasion—a sanding of the skin—because I would like a smoother complexion.

Similarly, a 52-year-old, middle-class woman stated: "I would never consider anything like Botox. I don't believe in injecting poison in my body. You know, it concerns me that some of this stuff just hasn't been around long enough to see what the long-term effects are." Indeed, Botox was one product that was ridiculed more than any other by both the women who had used non-surgical cosmetic procedures and those who had not, and comments such as the following were very common:

> Oh, well, toxin, clostridium botulinum is the producer of the toxin. I worked in food poisoning [research lab] for a while and was very aware

of the toxic effects. And here we are putting one of the components in our faces. Eww! You know, I mean, cases where people die. Uh, you know, a five star restaurant—botulism in the mushrooms. So to me, that would be silly to put that in your face. (age 64, middle class)

Women who had had non-surgical procedures tended to make moral and physical distinctions between the types of products they had purchased and injectables, which they viewed disparagingly. For example, a 71-year-old, middle-class woman who had previously used microdermabrasion contended the following:

I wouldn't go near injections . . . to me, microdermabrasion is an extension of the pedicure, manicure. . . . Yeah I would never—I look at those injections and I really feel, what is wrong with these women? You know, what price beauty? Like I just am totally, totally mystified at the amount of pain women will now endure. So no injections. . . . I don't think I should be so hard in my judgment of them just because I personally wouldn't get into it. And by that, I mean the Botox and stuff. . . . But I think there is a big divide between that sort of thing and what I did.

Part of the distinction that the women made between their own use of non-surgical cosmetic procedures and the employment of injections had to do with their perceptions of the end products. Similar to their comments about the use of certain hair dyes, the women suggested that Botox produced particularly unnatural and undesirable results. For example, a 51-year-old, middle-class woman who worked as a nurse and who had had microdermabrasion in the past stated:

I've actually had patients who had Botox and they just don't look right. I had a patient the other day who was 69 and when I entered the waiting room to call her in, I couldn't see anybody who looked that age. There was this lady who looked like she was in her 50s and I called her and it was her. And I said, "Oh you look great!" But close up, she didn't! . . . She had no lines at all and her face was so stretched. It looked like a mask actually. It looked really odd.

Results that were readily apparent or that made the gap between a person's chronological age and their appearance too great, such as looking 50 at the age of 69, were deemed to have transgressed acceptable beauty work limits. In this way, the women argued that while one should strive to "look good for your age," as the physicians put it, one should be careful to not look unnatural, obviously altered, or fake, a topic that will be explored further in the next chapter. The emphasis on looking youthful by ridding the face of wrinkles was delimited by social norms concerning age-appropriate appearances that made the navigation of beauty work options simultaneously a moral requirement and a justification for harsh criticism and further devaluation.

## SUMMARY AND CONCLUSIONS

In this chapter, I have examined the ways in which wrinkles were viewed and experienced by physicians and older women. In particular, I have explored how the medicalization of facial creases influenced older women's perceptions of their aging faces and their experiences of growing older. For physicians, the treatment of wrinkles using non-surgical cosmetic procedures was the consumer-driven, logical, and scientific response to what were unquestioningly accepted as negative, physical blemishes that required and justified medical intervention. These physical failings were perceived to be the particular concern, if not fate, of women as a result of biological differences (e.g., women having thinner skin than men) and women's larger focus on and investment in their appearances more generally as compared to men. While some of the physicians acknowledged the pressure women faced with respect to appearance work and achieving idealized beauty, they largely attributed women's greater tendency to seek out aesthetic medicine to their inferior biology, their innate vanity, or unquestioned social norms. In this way, the physicians contributed to the social construction of gendered and aging bodies as well as to gendered and age-based oppression. Failing to recognize their own power and privilege as predominantly young, White, male doctors in a system that heightened women's anxiety and sense of social and bodily failure and ultimately contributed to their oppression, the physicians were complicit in the entrenchment of older women's social devaluation.

At the same time, the physicians' suggestion that consumers of non-surgical cosmetic procedures were individuals who tended to be healthier and more concerned with self-care underscored the intermingling of ageism and healthism in discourses about appearance. Like the anti-aging practitioners in Mykytyn's (2006) study, the physicians accepted and perpetuated ageist discourses that devalued the aging body and privileged the possession of youthfulness as a chronological state, an indicator of health, as well as the product of medical inscription on the previously deficient body. Consequently, appearance became a gauge of an individual's success at not aging and at leading a health-promoting lifestyle as well as the key means of assigning social currency defined in terms of youthfulness and entitlement to the participatory rights of citizenship. Like Mykytyn's (2006) anti-aging practitioners who embraced "a scientific revolutionary identity" (p. 643), the physicians perceived their job to be an essential part of the fight against aging (and thereby against poor health) as they worked to ameliorate the inevitable flaws that resulted from physical aging within the limits of an individual's chronological age and their willingness to engage in aesthetic medicine. Notably, the physicians prescribed and personally adhered to a doctrine of anti-aging living that included attention to nutrition, physical activity, and, most importantly, investment in appearance. In this way, through their personal and professional pursuits, the physicians were ultimately writing their own oppression and descent into societal obsolescence.

Highly intelligent and articulate, the physicians were also skillful vendors who frequently and subtly wove into their conversations with me unsolicited assessments of what they perceived to be my facial and bodily flaws and their suggestions for how best to treat these unnecessary appearance defects. Despite my education and my critical feminist stance with respect to aesthetic medicine, I was surprised and dismayed by how easily shaken my self-confidence was in the wake of such authoritative but understated condemnation of my outer facade. Flaws I never knew existed, such as my apparently uneven eyebrows and the facial discoloration that was part of my pregnancy at the time of the interview were suddenly made painfully, if not shamefully, visible in the panopticon (Foucault, 1979) created by the physicians' casual evaluations. Such revelations made the power of the physicians devastatingly clear, and I was left to wonder how women who were already convinced that their appearances were in need of medical intervention when they entered these physicians' offices might be even more profoundly impacted than I had been.

Although physicians have a powerful influence on how women experience and perceive their bodies, women's attitudes toward their wrinkles and to aesthetic medicine were varied. Conducted before the development of non-surgical cosmetic procedures, Study #1 entailed interviews with women who had an average age of 77 in 1999. The women were divided in their attitudes toward wrinkles; half expressed displeasure with their facial creases and the other half conveyed feelings of acceptance, if not resignation. The women who disliked their wrinkles tended to endorse cosmetic surgery as an acceptable option, although they indicated that they themselves would be unlikely to pursue surgical intervention, primarily because of the financial costs such measures entailed. Those women who advocated acceptance often described their facial creases as a normative part of growing older to which individuals should be reconciled even if they were not fond of or pleased with their wrinkles. These women frequently were opposed to cosmetic surgery, which they viewed as a vain and needlessly risky response to the inevitability of grower older and becoming less attractive. At the same time, many of the women in Study #1 downplayed the importance of wrinkles, pointing to the greater social and physical impacts of the loss of health and functional abilities. While they rarely expressed pleasure with their wrinkles and were aware that extant beauty ideals progressively disqualified them from being considered physically attractive, the women noted that loss of physical abilities was ultimately more devastating to their social engagement, quality of life, and level of exclusion.

Study #2 involved interviews with baby boomers in the wake of the formal approval of Botox and the boom in the development of a myriad of non-surgical aesthetic products. These women were decidedly negative in their attitudes toward wrinkles, which they considered to be unattractive, undesirable, and signifiers of internal decline and impending death. While half of the study participants had previously tried non-surgical cosmetic procedures and the other half had not, the majority held a very dim view of cosmetic surgery, which was considered to be extreme and unnecessarily risky. In contrast, most of the women were open to using one or more non-surgical cosmetic procedure in the future irrespective of their past experiences of the products. Indeed, even those women who had been profoundly dissatisfied with the results of previous non-surgical cosmetic procedures indicated a willingness to try new and different products because the perceived benefits of looking younger outweighed the health and appearance risks of the treatments going awry. Additionally, these women hung on to the hope that the new products and procedures would have increasing appearance dividends and decreasing health hazards as physicians and pharmaceutical companies continued to push the boundaries of science.

Nevertheless, the women were less comfortable with medical beauty interventions that transgressed the outer boundaries of the body, as in the case of injectable fillers and Botox injections. Botox was perceived to be especially risky because of its derivation from a neurotoxin. Additionally, Botox was vilified because of its association with unnatural and disingenuous looking outcomes. These views reflected broader societal criticisms that are often couched in humor and particularly target Botox. Indeed, Botox is often disparaged for its apparent erasure of human emotion from the face as muscles are rendered immobile and the individual is perceived to lose the ability to either frown or smile. Ironically, this latter criticism stands in sharp opposition to the women's stated motivations for using Botox, namely to rid the face of an excess of negative emotion denoted by the presence of wrinkles. Whereas some women argued that a total lack of emotional expression as a result of the use of Botox appeared phony and bizarre, consumers of the product maintained that the presence of "mad lines" or "crabby creases" were indicative of oldness and ugliness, as feminine beauty was defined in terms of a docile and disciplined body (Bordo, 2003) and the possession of a pleasing demeanor and a youthful, smooth countenance.

The equation of wrinkles with negative emotion and, therefore, with oldness warrants further comment, as there appeared to be a marked evolution in the complexity of the meanings attributed to wrinkles in Study #1 and Study #2. Prior to the development of non-surgical cosmetic procedures, the women in Study #1 spoke about wrinkles as a general and undifferentiated category of facial creases. However, in the second study, the women's narratives became laced with assertions that particular wrinkles were acceptable while others were especially abhorrent. Specifically, wrinkles around the eyes were said to denote character and laughter and thereby were tolerable, if not appealing, while wrinkles in the forehead and around the mouth were associated with negative emotion and oldness. The demarcation of acceptable and unacceptable wrinkles paralleled developments in aesthetic medicine. To date, there have not been any non-surgical cosmetic procedures invented that eliminate "laughter lines," "character lines," or "crow's feet." In contrast, Botox injections and injectable fillers target the now much-maligned creases in the brow and around the mouth. In this way, the construction and embracement of two categories of wrinkles, one with relatively positive associations and one with pejorative connotations, reflected the limits of technological innovation.

Simultaneously, one of the most visible indicators of aging and advanced age and an aspect of physical appearance that requires extensive investments of time and money to eliminate, wrinkles are emblematic of the convergence of anti-aging technology, age and gender relations, and healthist discourses. According to the hierarchical binary of old and not-old, the young are thought to embody youthfulness, healthiness, and happiness while the aged are assumed to be disagreeable, frail, and unfulfilled. As pharmaceutical companies continue to develop products and physicians and other health care professionals skillfully sell their wares, it seems inevitable that additional wrinkles will be redefined and new facial flaws will be identified as the face is mined for all of its potential commercial worth. Consequently, the scope of women's dissatisfaction with their aging faces will continue to grow to match the pace and range of the developing aesthetic medical technology. Within this growing terrain of beauty work, the moral imperative to attend to one's wrinkles so as to appear healthy, young, and attractive will only continue to build in intensity even as the battle to appear young is ultimately destined to fail. Moreover, this war against time will become increasingly fraught with moral overtones as the aged-looking face is taken to denote insufficient personal self-care, irresponsibility, and evidence of a lack of common decency. While physicians and pharmaceutical companies will reap unending financial rewards, it is women, particularly older women, who will fail a little more each day as their appearances increasingly deviate from unattainable beauty ideals.

## NOTES

1. Please see chapter 1 for specific details regarding the sample and design of this study.

2. For reviews of the history of anti-aging medicine, please see the following articles: J. R. Fishman, R. H. Binstock, and M. A. Lambrix, "Anti-aging Science: The Emergence, Maintenance, and Enhancement of a Discipline," *Journal of Aging Studies* 22, no. 3 (2008): 295–303; J. R. Fishman, R. A. Settersten Jr., and M. A. Flatt, "In the Vanguard of Biomedicine? The Curious and Contradictory Case of Anti-Ageing Medicine," *Sociology of Health and Illness* 32, no. 2 (2010): 197–210; C. E. Mykytyn, "Medicalizing the Optimal: Anti-aging Medicine and the Quandary of Intervention," *Journal of Aging Studies* 22, no. 3 (2008): 313–21; C. E. Mykytyn, "Anti-aging Medicine: A Patient/Practitioner Movement to Redefine Aging," *Social Science and Medicine* 62, no. 3 (2006), 643–53.

# 5

## Imaging Aging:
## Media Messages and the
## Perspectives of Older Women

Leiss, Kline, Jhally, and Botterill (2005) have stated:

> Advertising is not just a business expenditure undertaken in the hope of moving some merchandise off the store shelves, but is rather an integral part of modern culture. Its creations appropriate and transform a vast range of symbols and ideas; its unsurpassed communicative powers recycle cultural models and references back through the networks of social interactions. This venture is unified by the discourse through and about objects, which bonds together images of persons, products, and well-being. (p. 5)

While advertising seeks to persuade consumers to not only purchase commodities, but also to embrace certain ideologies, individuals are not without power and ultimately decide which products to buy and which meanings to accept, reject, or transmute. Nevertheless, Leiss et al. (2005) maintain: "That consumers exercise limited choice in the market or see through advertising persuasive strategies does not imply that advertising's social communication is benign or inconsequential" (p. 13). Indeed, while the media reflect and reinforce dominant ideologies concerning the body, aging, and gender (Calasanti, 2007; Laws, 1995), these constructs are deeply and strategically embedded in the images and text of advertising (Leiss et al., 2005), often to the detriment of women's social currency and sense of well-being (Bordo, 2003; Kilbourne, 1999; Wolf, 1991).

Nowhere is the privileging of youthfulness in cultural ideals of beauty more apparent than in the mass media. Hollywood actresses and print and television advertisements depict feminine beauty as the sole purview of young, predominantly White, physically fit, thin yet buxom women. In contrast, older women are largely invisible and negatively portrayed in the movies, print advertisements, and television programming (Bazzini et al., 1997; Carrigan & Szmigin, 2000; de Luce, 2001; Harwood & Roy, 1999; Healey & Ross, 2002; Kessler et al., 2004; Vernon et al., 1990). Further, the signs of physical aging are usually airbrushed away in print ads, used as fodder for comedic story lines in television and movies, and exemplified as the enemy against which individuals should fight using a myriad of beauty products and interventions (Calasanti & Slevin, 2001; Featherstone & Wernick, 1995; Markson & Taylor, 2000; Wolf, 1991).

At the same time, the Dove Campaign for Real Beauty has sparked further debate about the positioning of older women in the media and the centrality of beauty work to the construction of gendered and aged bodies. This campaign entailed a series of photographs of women who were supposed to represent average female citizens by virtue of their size, shape, age, race, and various bodily imperfections. The advertisements that used images of older women asked the reader to define the photographs as either "wrinkled" or "wonderful" and "gray" or "gorgeous." Well-known feminist psychoanalyst Susie Orbach (2009) was a consultant and co-originator of the advertising campaign. While cultural theorists such as Cortese (2008) have commended the advertisements for being a strong and effective impetus for social change, some feminist sociologists, such as Leavy (2007), have argued that the campaign is an example of "the resistive potential of popular culture" (p. 246).

In contrast, Dye (2009) asserts that "the focus on individual concerns and experiences within the Dove campaign overshadows the notion of collective resistance to Western beauty standards" (p. 116). Dye (2009) also points out the contradictions inherent in the fact that Dove's parent company, Unilever, also promotes the Axe line of products for men using "fantasy babes," or models who fit the dominant and oppressive beauty ideal. Dye (2009) and Johnston and Taylor (2008) further contend that the campaign is ultimately about the marketing of beauty products, including those that adhere to anti-aging discourses despite their "Pro Age" product line name, and is thereby underscored by the message that even "real women" must ultimately engage in beauty work and discipline their bodies with a variety of cosmetics and lotions in order to be feminine and socially valued. Feminist writer and activist, Jennifer L. Pozner (2005), puts it this way:

> Despite the company's continued and commendable intent to expand notions of female beauty to include the non-skinny and non-white, Dove's attempts are profoundly limited by a product line that comes with its own underlying philosophy: cellulite is unsightly, women's natural aging process is shameful, and flabby thighs are flawed and must be fixed . . . oh, so conveniently by Dove's newest lotion.

Regardless of the controversies surrounding Dove's alternative images of beauty, older women continue to be marginalized in the mainstream media, and the dominant messages concerning aging are that it is the ultimate failure. Media imagery suggests that older women are unattractive and undesirable living examples of everything younger adults should strive against with all available means within consumer culture. Elucidating the complexities of media messages and women's responses to the prevailing anti-aging discourses, I examine the language of print ads in five women's magazines as well as the perspectives of older women concerning the social construction and depiction of beauty in the mass media more generally. Specifically, I discuss how ageist messages pertaining to beauty are both subtly and blatantly used to market anti-aging beauty products. Next, I use data from my interviews with older women to examine their perspectives on the face of beauty as it is presented in the media and the concomitant impact of these images on their sense of identity, well-being, and beauty work choices. To that end, I build on the women's general feelings about their bodies as well as their attitudes toward wrinkles and non-surgical cosmetic procedures and discuss beauty work more broadly and as a response to ageism.

## BEAUTY AND AGING IN PRINT ADVERTISEMENTS

I begin by presenting my findings from Study #5, in which I conducted a content analysis of anti-aging-related print advertisements that appeared in *Harper's Bazaar, Ladies' Home Journal, More, O: The Oprah Magazine*, and *Vogue* between July 2004 and July 2005. Of the 293 advertisements that were coded, 230 (78 percent) of the advertisements made direct references to anti-aging discourses in order to market their products and 198 (86 percent) of these were for products specifically targeting the face and the treatment of facial wrinkles. For example, many of the advertisements claimed that the use of their specific products would result in younger-looking facial skin, which was portrayed as an essential element of feminine beauty. Lancome Renergie Microlift was purported to have the following effect: "My skin's youthful definition visibly returns. I look years younger." Similarly, the advertisements for RoC Retinol Correxion claimed that the product "Gives 10 years back to the look of your skin," and Derma-Gen Anti-wrinkle Patches with Ultimate Swiss Peel System was marketed in this way: "Now more than ever, a faster and safer way to look years younger." The emphasis on youthfulness was further underscored by the choice of models pictured in the various advertisements. Although the models typically appeared to be between 20 and 35, the advertisements often suggested that the women's appearances belied their true chronological ages, thanks to the use of the products. With flawless and wrinkle-free skin, perfectly coiffed and colored hair, chic makeup, and fashionable attire, the women exuded confidence, glamour, and sexual appeal, which were suggested to be the purview of the young and not the old or aging.

Many of the advertisements also used the phrase *anti-aging* to market their products: "Introducing the most revolutionary anti-aging product ever created" (Hydroderm Fast-Acting Wrinkle Reducer); "This anti-aging phenomenon helps lift away the look of deep wrinkles faster than ever before" (Estee Lauder Perfectionist [CP+] with Poly-Collagen Peptides); and "The answer for anti-aging is easier than you think" (Neutrogena Advanced Solutions). The suggestion that one should be against or "anti" later life and the physical inevitability of growing older was further underscored by the language of aggression and resistance in some of the marketing campaigns: "Fight seven signs of aging" and "It's a one-two punch in the fight against aging" (Olay Total Effects 7x and Night Firming Creams); "New Aveeno Positively Radiant Anti-wrinkle Cream is clinically proven to fight wrinkles and even tone" (Aveeno Positively Radiant Anti-wrinkle Cream); and "Change the destiny of your skin with groundbreaking, targeted Cell Vector technology that helps re-ignite its natural age-fighting ability with stunning accuracy and speed" (Estee Lauder Future Perfect Anti-wrinkle Radiance Moisturizer SPF 15).

At the same time, some of the product names strongly resembled non-surgical cosmetic procedures and/or used pseudoscientific language to market and legitimate their products. For example, the product "Bo-Hylurox" sounds like a combination of Botox and hyaluronic acid in both name and purported function: "Anew Clinical's exclusive Bo-Hylurox technology targets hard-to-treat lines with two treatments, one to relax and another to fill." Bearing a strong resemblance to Restylane, "Resystane" was marketed as the active ingredient of Lancome's Resolution Wrinkle Concentrate: "With Resystane this serum helps to reinforce skin. Skin is more resilient against wrinkles and dermo-creases." Other products said they contained such elements as "Poly-Collagen Peptides," "Retinol AHA complex with age-fighting DMEA," "Glycolic acid blended with Urea," "collagen complex," and "Celluzyme." What was once referred to as a cream is now described as a "an anti-wrinkle serum that stimulates collagen growth," "revolutionary, patented collagen infusion technology," an "anti-aging phenomenon," and "groundbreaking, targeted Cell Vector technology," which collectively connote scientific innovation and legitimacy and draw on the publicity and value attributed to science more generally and recognized non-surgical cosmetic procedures more specifically. The underlying message in these advertisements is that since "recent scientific breakthroughs" have made it possible to halt or even reverse the aging process, rational and enlightened individuals will respond to their moral obligation to engage in various health promotion strategies and will do their utmost to look and, therefore, be young.

Additionally, the product jingles frequently alleged that their products were cheaper and safer than surgical or non-surgical cosmetic procedures: "If you're thinking about lasers, peels or shots, consider this gentle, retinol-free alternative" (Estee Lauder Perfectionist Correcting Serum for Lines/Wrinkles); "Cosmetic procedures involving chemicals and lasers can provide serious skin improvement. Olay Regenerist gives you dramatic results without resorting to drastic measures" (Olay Regenerist Daily Regenerating Serum); "For every woman who says no to Botox" and "Now, triumph over wrinkles without toxins, lasers or injections" (Estee Lauder Perfectionist [CP+] with Poly-Collagen Peptides); "A smoother, younger complexion, less irritation, fewer wrinkles, and faster results—all without expensive (and painful) peels, implants, or injections" (Strivectin SD); and "You don't want liposuction—just an at-home alternative. . . . No pain, no lipo—just lifted spirits" (Avon Anew Clinical Lift and Tuck).

Some advertisements even went so far as to suggest that their products were superior to surgical and non-surgical cosmetic procedures with respect to overall effectiveness: "Many researchers believe less invasive cosmetic alternatives are better than Botox. That's because topical creams and gels offer gradual, continual results, while the effects of injections, facial peels, and dermabrasions wear off" (Strivectin SD); "The revolutionary new Anti-Aging Cream for the entire body and Reparative Formula for the face, goes where Botox can't" (Dr. Michelle Copeland Skin Care); "Hydroderm is the only anti-aging product in the world that delivers a full collagen molecule directly to the epidermis" (Hydroderm Fast-Acting Wrinkle Reducer); "Together, Idealist and Idealist Micro-D perform up to 74% better than microdermabrasion at reducing the look of pores and up to 56% better at improving the evenness of skin tone" (Estee Lauder Idealist Skin Refinisher and Micro-D Deep Thermal Refinisher). A few advertisements further touted their products as either more natural or less expensive than non-surgical cosmetic procedures: "This natural alternative to Botox is safe, effective and available only for $39.95" (Royal Touch Anti-wrinkle Serum).

Taken as a whole, these anti-aging advertisements compel readers to consume products so as to achieve a "beautiful," "brilliant," "dramatically improved," "luminous," "more resilient," "radiant," "refined," and "stunning" appearance that is "healthier looking" and that has "youthful definition." Moreover, the possession of "visible signs of aging," "deep wrinkles," "expression lines," "loss of elasticity," "poorly defined facial contours," "the visible effects of time," "dull, tired skin," and "dermo-creases" are depicted as unappealing, or even worthy of ridicule. Consequently, aging and old bodies are simultaneously the epitome of ugliness and the product of poor consumption patterns on the part of the consumer. In this way, individuals can and should choose to resist aging and "turn back the clock" by engaging in beauty work regimens and actively disciplining their bodies and their faces.

## OLDER WOMEN REFLECT ON THE BODY AND FACE OF BEAUTY IN THE MEDIA

When asked to reflect on the beauty embodied by female media icons, including Hollywood actresses, runway models, advertisement personas, or television talk show hosts, most of the women I interviewed over the years were highly critical. To begin, the women often soundly rejected contemporary female media personalities as exemplars of ideal female bodies primarily because of their tendency to be exceedingly thin. The women used words and phrases such as "absolutely ridiculous," "anorexic," "appalling," "awful," "a damn disgrace," "not natural," "not normal," "repellent," "terrible," "too thin," "sickly," "ugly," and "walking anorexics" to refer to the body shapes, specifically the weights, of fashion models and media stars. The women made comments similar to those of a 61-year-old, middle-class woman:

> They all look like they need a square meal. I'm sorry, but I don't see them as attractive at all. I don't know why we're obsessed with super thin. . . . This obsession . . . does not meet my recommendations at all. It's not something I would do.

However, some women were also sympathetic to the plight of individuals in the media spotlight who were perceived to be under enormous pressure to meet externally imposed beauty standards. A

71-year-old, middle-class woman who had used microdermabrasion in the past asserted the following:

> It's just part of the age where looking good, especially if they're on television or they are interviewers—you know the pressure must be intense to look good and keep your looks. I mean supermodels and all this—you know there's somebody waiting to take your place if you're not there.

In contrast to the contemporary emphasis on excessive thinness and their own stated displeasure with their weights and persistent use of dieting to discipline their own bodies, the women argued that shapely bodies were more desirable and indicative of feminine beauty. A 56-year-old, middle-class woman stated: "I think women that are curvy rather than really slim are more attractive. I think women who are more voluptuous—like ripe—that's the kind of body that I think is great." To demonstrate their meaning, some women referenced contemporary personalities who ranged in slimness but who embodied a shapeliness that was not naturally possible in an extremely thin body. For example, the women referred to Jennifer Lopez, Queen Latifah, and Britney Spears as examples of individuals whom they considered to be beautiful. Another 56-year-old, middle-class woman revealed the following:

> My ideal body would be Britney Spears. Well, wouldn't you die to look like that? She has a flat stomach and she's got lots of curves. She's not skinny by any stretch of the imagination so she's got a very sexy body.

While some provided examples of current media icons in their definitions and examples of feminine beauty, most of the women tended to refer to movie stars from earlier decades such as Ava Gardner, Betty Grable, Catherine Deneuve, Bo Derek, Grace Kelly, Joanne Woodward, Jane Russell, Sophia Loren, and Elizabeth Taylor. In particular, Marilyn Monroe was the most often cited example of a body shape and size that was highly esteemed and contrasted with extremes of thinness, embodied by the likes of Twiggy, Kate Moss, Paris Hilton, or Gwyneth Paltrow. It is important to point out that the ages of the women in my studies have ranged from 50 to 90+ and the studies have spanned a 10-year period. Thus, the women's choices of ideal movie actresses spanned a similar time range and included a mixture of body shapes and sizes, including voluptuous and less curvaceous bodies. Nevertheless, the women tended to indicate a preference for shapely female bodies over that of what a 51-year-old, middle-class woman described as "the straight up and down figure that seems to be most popular now."

At the same time, many of the women commented on how the beauty standards had noticeably shifted over their lifetimes. A 64-year-old, middle-class woman contended the following:

> If you look at the old movies, I mean, Jane Russell was our idea of beauty. I think girls were a lot fatter and they were beautiful. Like, Marilyn Monroe was quite chubby at times, and Jane Russell, I mean— they had huge breasts! They were definitely heavier. The girls now are so thin. I mean, like Gwyneth Paltrow, they are anorexic. Just skinny, skinny arms, skinny legs, you know?

As well as shifting from privileging curvier bodies to esteeming thinness, the women noted that beautiful bodies had also come to be equated with physical fitness and surgical enhancements. A 56-year-old, middle-class woman opined:

> Ideals have changed. If you think back to the movies that we watched as teenagers with, say, Annette Funicello. She was not thin. They had little pot tummies. And that was the ideal. And now it's kind of like rail-thin. And the ab thing—everybody's got to have those abs. Even the girls— they've all got these skinny stomachs and they all have breasts and if they don't have breasts naturally, they put them in surgically.

Thus, the changes that had occurred in feminine beauty ideals had often been to the detriment of the women's perceived social currencies and approximation of physical attractiveness standards. A 60-year-old, lesbian, middle-class woman maintained:

> When I was growing up, Marilyn Monroe was the epitome of beauty. She had a figure and, of course, I did not, in comparison. So, I always felt I was lacking because I didn't look like Marilyn Monroe. But as I got older and looked more like Marilyn Monroe, the standard became Twiggy, and now 14-year-old models that are very thin are the standard. So now, because I have more of a figure, I'm still out of fashion. And the whole thing makes me just think, "Oh isn't this ridiculous?!"

In their identification of female media stars that they admired, the women's internalization of youthfulness as a requirement for beauty became readily apparent. Rarely referring to older actresses or media icons as examples of beautiful women, the women tended to talk about young media personalities. Moreover, the women's narratives concerning older individuals such as Jane Fonda, Goldie Hawn, Helen Mirren, Susan Sarandon, and Meryl Streep were ambivalent. For example, a 65-year-old middle-class woman had this to say:

> Helen Mirren looks pretty good. She isn't beautiful but she looks fine. I mean, she has her lines and all the rest of it. . . . Also Susan Sarandon is a pretty fortunate woman in that she has this pretty gorgeous body and face but I'm mad at her now because of the TV and magazine ads she's been doing for Revlon. . . . I've lost respect for her. She's not poor. How can she do that? I always thought that she was one of the few women in Hollywood who thought character meant more than appearance.

Therefore, the women either stated that older Hollywood actresses or television personalities were attractive irrespective of their obviously aging appearances or the women alleged that the stars had lost their credibility because of their use of beauty interventions to hide or remove wrinkles, sagging skin, and other visible indicators of their age. Furthermore, the women directly asserted that beauty was equivalent to youthful bodies and appearances, as they made comments similar to those of a 51-year-old, middle-class woman who asserted:

> Youth is more attractive . . . young people is where there's fashion. Young people are where there's fun. I guess it's important for anybody who is not young to think they should either be young or they don't count. If you put it into a sentence—be young or you're not counted.

However, the majority of the women also argued that many of the contemporary female media stars appeared "unnatural," "fake," and even "ugly" as a result of cosmetic surgery and various beauty interventions that had made obvious changes in their appearances. The women made comments similar to those of a 56-year-old, middle-class woman who used injectable fillers, laser skin treatments, and chemical peels to fight the signs of aging in her own face:

I think you're more pleasing to look at if you look natural. I mean, you see people, the movie stars, where it's very obvious they've had cosmetic surgery. They're pulled and twisted and they start to get distorted looking. Their faces start to look weird.

Emphasizing the importance of looking natural and aging gracefully (Hurd Clarke & Griffin, 2007a), many of the women conveyed cautionary tales using movie stars who they perceived to have excessive or poorly done cosmetic surgeries, including Pamela Anderson, Joan Collins, Michael Jackson, Priscilla Presley, Joan Rivers, Burt Reynolds, and Elizabeth Taylor. For example, a 62-year-old woman who had a very limited income maintained:

I think the most shocking picture I've ever seen is one of Goldie Hawn. . . . Now she was just plain butt ugly. She has been putting that junk, whatever she's shooting, into her face for years. And man oh man! I thought to myself, "There's the end result of people getting injections."

Similarly, a 52-year-old, upper-class woman contended:

You don't want to look like Joan Rivers. Or if you saw Priscilla Presley, you'd throw up. . . . Oh God! I don't know what she did. She has the biggest claim to sue her plastic surgeon. I don't know who she went with. She just looks terrible. She's starting to look like the "Cat Lady."

When it came to print advertisements, the women's feelings were even more conflicted. Even as they expressed awareness that the commercials and magazine photographs were airbrushed, digitally altered, and staged, many of the women described feeling pressured by various forms of advertising to consume beauty interventions and to work to discipline and alter their bodies so as to appear more desirable. The women argued that part of the pressure that they experienced came from the ubiquitous nature of the media messages concerning ideal feminine beauty, especially those embodied in TV and magazine advertisements for beauty products. Asserting sentiments such as "the influence of the media is huge," the women used words and phrases like "bombarded," "pushed," and "pressurized to look good all the time" to describe their feelings about the extant media messages. The women also expressed anger and dismay at the ageist messages conveyed in some of the advertisements, such as those for Botox, which suggested that in preparation for their daughters' wedding days, mothers should get non-surgical cosmetic procedures so that their pictures preserved in albums would not be a source of embarrassment. Additionally, the women suggested that the nature and number of the advertisements and media messages combined to be "psychologically and emotionally manipulating," as a 52-year-old, upper-class woman put it. A 71-year-old, middle-class woman who had used microdermabrasion in the past described her experiences this way:

> You cannot get away from it whether it's television or movies or videos or magazines. They get into your psyche and somehow you are not quite up to it. You get these images of perfection and you're always found wanting . . . and you internalize that . . . and you just can't turn it off . . . so we're being manipulated all the time.

Similarly, a 58-year-old, lesbian, middle-class woman contended the following:

> Every page you look at, every piece of advertising is all about this: People are scared of getting old and looking old. The pressure is so big that to avoid it or to kick it is hard. I think we're all affected in some way . . . we internalize that we don't look good unless we do things. So the more you're told that, the more you start to believe it and it becomes a part of you. The message is so strong that you internalize that "This is what I need to do." . . . It's the same kind of message we got when we were young—you know, that girls are dumb and we can't do math . . . so now I just can't do math. I can do a little bit but because I was told that I couldn't think around math—that it was a boy's thing—I internalized it so much to the point that it became a problem. I think this is the same with the cosmetic industry and the diet industry and the fitness industry and all that.

In this way, the constant bombardment of media messages asserting the need to be thin, young, and wrinkle-free reflected and reinforced sexist and ageist ideologies that the women encountered, negotiated, and embraced in their everyday interactions. The women experienced a limited sense of being able to resist these demeaning meanings, which left them feeling constantly in need of self-improvement, woefully lacking, and the target of oppressive societal surveillance

(Bartky, 1998; Bordo, 2003). A 65-year-old, middle-class woman described how she perceived that the media had negatively influenced her sense of identity and well-being:

> The media has always impacted on me. I've never been able to ignore it or distance myself from it. I've incorporated the values of our mainstream media and so it's been a continual struggle for me to counter those values. . . . When I look through all these women's magazines and see all of these advertisements for wrinkle creams and the amount of cosmetic surgeons there are out there now, I am just absolutely appalled at what's going on. Really . . . But for some weird reason, I'm drawn to the messages in the media, and when I'm in a grocery store, I will pick up these trashy magazines and leaf through them . . . and they're all about diets and wrinkle creams . . . and I go to movies and I have learned what is acceptable and what is not acceptable in our culture. So that when I look in the mirror and I see the physical deterioration—um, you know, the lights go on and I think you shouldn't have these things.

Describing the ideologies underpinning the advertisements as a vortex that was dragging them in, the women were also aware of their own culpability in the reinforcement of ageist and sexist cultural values through their own unwillingness to reject the products and the meanings associated with them. Indeed, many of these women suggested that they were knowingly "sucked in," as they frequently put it, by the promises of the advertisements and consequently continued to purchase and try various products. For example, a 51-year-old, upper-class woman revealed the following:

> I try everything. I mean, I don't believe all these advertisements—you know, "Reduces lines by 50% in two weeks." I mean after 51 years in the sun it's not going to do that. And I've tried every wrinkle cream available and I've seen really no difference actually. So I don't believe all these ads. You know, often they are using these women with these flawless skins, and nobody has skin like that, right. And it's probably very short lived, you know, they cover their spots and things. . . . So I don't believe these things but I still buy them of course.

Thus, even though they disputed and disbelieved the claims of advertisements, the women were unwilling to give up the hope that the next product or beauty intervention that they tried would render their countenances more youthful and, therefore, more attractive. Having internalized ageist discourses, the women embraced media messages in the hope that the products would help them to avoid ageism and, ultimately, social exclusion. Additionally, despite their awareness of the contrived nature of advertising and modelling more generally, the women continued to measure themselves and their beauty work efforts against the models, products, and services being proffered in the media and upheld by their peers.

However, a few women reported that they did not feel influenced or pressured by advertisements and media messages. For example, a 72-year-old woman who had a very limited income and who used chemical peels stated: "Maybe other women feel pressured to look younger because they see too much on TV or read about it. I don't feel pressured. I do it for me. That's not pressure." In this case, the decision to purchase cosmetics and try non-surgical cosmetic procedures was perceived to be a personal choice that culminated in enhanced physical attractiveness, self-esteem, and personal pleasure. Additionally, the importance of striving to be youthful in appearance was unquestioningly embraced as a legitimate, positive, and requisite outcome of beauty work. Ironically, the notion of "doing it for me" reflected the language of many marketing jingles of the advertisements, particularly a prominent Botox campaign, which urged women to pamper themselves as much as they nurtured others. Thus, using anti-aging beauty products was positioned as a much-deserved form of self-care, and, therefore, as a vital, if not entitled, aspect of doing gender and femininity (West & Zimmerman, 1987).

Other women actively tried to avoid advertisements for beauty products so as to minimize the personal pressure and sense of inadequacy the various marketing strategies generated. For example, a 56-year-old, lower-class woman reported:

> I'm ad aversive. I don't read them. I don't notice them. They're sort of there, and maybe they're in subliminally, but I don't notice them. I don't notice ads period, unless I'm actually looking for something. I record everything I watch on TV, so I never see advertisements. I don't get the local paper and I stopped buying magazines because they have too many ads in them.

These women found the ageist and sexist messages embedded in the advertisements to be particularly disturbing, as expressed by a 60-year-old, lesbian, middle-class woman who maintained: "I tend not to read ads just because I can't   it makes me upset."

However, several women indicated that they not only ignored advertising, they felt immune to the persuasive marketing tactics employed by the media as well as to the broader cultural imperative to do gender through beauty work. For example, a 60-year-old, upper-class woman asserted that in addition to not paying attention to advertising, she was "not easily swayed or influenced." She went on to state the following:

> There's a lot of stuff and products and whatever but I don't see a need for them. . . . I guess appearance has never been a priority in my life. I mean maybe if when I was young I'd been taught to wear all this makeup and do my nails and all of the kind of thing—maybe I would be more tuned into it, and feel the need to do that to be acceptable but I don't.

When queried as to how she had managed to resist the influence of the media, this woman continued:

> I don't see it as resistance. It's just that it isn't important. It doesn't have any priority for me. It doesn't make me feel any better so the outcome probably isn't worth the time. . . . Maybe that's because I didn't get married when I was young and gain a whole bunch of weight having kids, and that kind of thing, that I have not felt that pressure. . . . I've always more or less supported myself. . . . I've had a degree of independence and . . . I really, you know, I don't know why. Somewhere along the line I must have been told I was alright enough—that I was okay the way I was so that I didn't feel that need.

Similarly, a 61-year-old, middle-class woman suggested that while she had previously been influenced by advertisements and media messages, their influence on her behavior and self-esteem was now diminished:

> I guess I'm just less conscious of my appearance. I just don't think about it as much. I'm less likely to be influenced by TV or magazines. . . . It just doesn't feel that important to me anymore. I just want to feel healthy. . . . I just don't put that much thought into it anymore. . . . I mean, in my

early 20s, you know, maybe I wanted to be more attractive in terms of dating or things like that. Or men—or that type of thing. And now I just don't, really.

This woman maintained that physical fitness, health, and relationships, particularly the one with her male partner of 30 years, were the focus of her attention and personal efforts.

## "AGING IS A SERIOUS PROBLEM": WOMEN, AGEISM DISCOURSES, AND BEAUTY WORK

In addition to critiquing Hollywood beauty ideals, many of the individuals I interviewed contended that what was considered to be an acceptable face of aging was becoming increasingly narrow in society and concomitantly in the media. A 68-year-old, middle-class woman who had had laser skin resurfacing as well as microdermabrasion had this to say: "When you look in a magazine and so on, there's that kind of feeling like, you're not allowed to have old people anymore—you know, you can be old but you can't show your age kind of thing." Similarly, a 55-year-old, middle-class woman asserted:

> I know there's this big thing about "old is beautiful" and everything like this but yet I still think that the people who are promoting "old is beautiful" are trying to make elderly people look young and then saying that those older people that look young are the beautiful ones. I think that's such a shame because, you know, you can be beautiful without having to look 20. And I just think, well, here's this Susan Sarandon, you know, I mean, what is she? She's got to be my age, if not older and yet she looks younger and like she's had some face-lifts. . . . What a shame that the ideal is young as opposed to being old and wise. What a shame. What a reflection on our society that we don't see the beauty in aging. Why isn't aging beautiful? . . . It's just a darn right shame that our society has not recognized that. I hope someday it will.

In this way, the women were acutely aware of the societal discourses that venerated youthfulness and only made oldness acceptable when one appeared youthful. While some women bemoaned the social devaluation of agedness and old-looking bodies, relatively few challenged and resisted the idea that only those older women who looked youthful could be considered attractive.

The women went on to say that the images in the media had translated into altered social expectations regarding the appearances of older women and that they themselves felt under increasing pressure to "not look their ages." The women made statements similar to those of a 71-year-old, middle-class woman who had used microdermabrasion who lamented the unobtainable nature of idealized beauty: "The whole bar has been set so high that, you know, at 50 you're still supposed to look 25 or 30." Additionally, the women noted that ageist messages were getting louder and more prolific with respect to the societal valuation of youthfulness and concepts of beauty and the concomitant equation of aging with deviance. For example, a 56-year-old, middle-class woman had this to say about advertisements for Botox and other anti-aging cosmetics and interventions:

> They suggest that somehow there's something wrong with the aging process. . . . I find it offensive that they'd market it that way. You know, it makes you start to question whether or not there's something wrong with you because you're not thinking about fixing yourself up. If I ain't broke, why do I want to fix myself?

This woman noted that advertisements served to make her and other women feel insecure and ambivalent about their bodies, which were constructed by the media and society at large as imperfect aberrations that warranted ongoing scrutiny and discipline (Bordo, 2003).

Societal discourses that positioned older women's bodies as deviant and abhorrent were most keenly felt in everyday interactions, which reinforced their devalued status and social exclusion. Similar to Holstein's (2001) personal reflections and experiences, some women contended that by looking their ages and thereby by diverging from extant beauty ideals, they experienced the sense that they were invisible to other people, particularly younger individuals and potential romantic partners. A 60-year-old, middle-class woman asserted:

> These days with such an emphasis on youth and beauty, it's somewhat of a detriment to be older. . . . We're such a youth-oriented society that

if you're not young and if you don't look young, you hear older women talk about the fact that they feel like they're invisible.

By virtue of looking and being older, the women were discounted by their younger counterparts and treated as invisible nonpersons who were unworthy of notice. This form of social exclusion was even more poignantly felt in the women's interactions with men, whose attentions were more easily garnered by younger women and who possessed the power to define them as sexually attractive individuals or nonentities. For example, a 52-year-old, lower-class woman reported:

> I've felt for the last 10 years that I'm completely invisible to men. I'm completely invisible with a tall, long-legged blonde in the room. Nobody even sees me. . . . That's why I don't like to go to very many events where people are in their 30s. I am invisible. I am not there. I get introduced to somebody but they're looking at somebody across the room. It's as though you're invisible. You're not there.

Similar to this participant, the women were acutely aware that their social currency and level of social inclusion were directly related to their appearances and to the appearance evaluations of others. Specifically, the women noted that sexist and ageist discourses and the physical realities of growing older were slowly robbing them of their personhood and their entitlement to social engagement and they were increasingly ignored by others. Beauty work became the one weapon that the women had to fight against their gradual and inevitable social annihilation. Thus, the women noted that in order to fight being rendered or considered invisible nonpersons, aging women had to attend to their appearances, particularly when on the dating scene or at work. When asked why she thought women engaged in various forms of beauty work, a single, 60-year-old, lesbian, middle-class woman clearly articulated the societal equation of acceptable appearances with personhood and social currency:

> They want someone to love them and they want to be accepted and they don't want to put up with ageism, which can be quite devastating. They want to still be people. . . . The women that I know—they're afraid that their partners won't want them if they're saggy or full of wrinkles. There's that fear of losing your partner to a younger woman. . . . We

won't love women if they're not lovely. Our society says that from the beginning. And for women who are older, we're invisible anyway. If you're considered ugly and old, ageism is awful and it's so prevalent.

At the same time, many of the women described having had a lifelong investment in appearance, which served to exacerbate their attention to the media, their willingness to try anti-aging products and treatments, and their sense of loss relative to the physical realities of growing older. For example, a 59-year-old middle-class woman who used Restylane injections stated:

> This is going to sound conceited but appearance is important to me because when I was young I was always very attractive, and because of that I got preferential treatment in a lot of things and preferential attention. I went through my life pretty much with that everywhere I went. I became quite used to it. That's why my vanity is really getting the better of me now, as I grow older. Because my appearance is going to be compared to what I was when I was young. So it's top priority to look as good as I can look and it always has been. When you're young and you're youthful and you're being told everywhere you go how attractive you are, it's very unsettling to look in the mirror and see any wrinkles appearing. When you see your beauty or your youthfulness disappearing, you become acutely aware that you're getting older.

A 63-year-old, upper-class woman who had used chemical peels and photo facials to reduce the evidence of chronological age on her face relayed her willingness to consume anti-aging products and discourses in terms of the perceived loss of the male gaze:

> I have always looked younger than my age. This is what's drawing me into the hope here with these new procedures because this is the first time in my life that I am starting to look old . . . which is hard. . . . I feel that I look like an old lady. If men at the bars saw me now, I don't think they would even talk to me because everything and everyone has to be young. . . . That's why I started the chemical peels and photo facials because they promised that you'll look younger.

Expressing awareness of her own socially tenuous situation with respect to her partner and her declining appearance resources, a 59-year-old, middle-class woman described her personal motivation for using non-surgical cosmetic procedures (Botox and collagen injections) in this way:

> My face is sagging and I'm at a stage in my life when I'm looking for a new partner hopefully to spend the rest of my life with. I've been going out with a guy who's 18 years older than I am, and we've been on and off for the past five or six years but I want somebody younger for a long-term relationship, possibly marriage. So, my appearance is very important to me right now. It's difficult to find men in my age range who are not going out with younger women. In this city there are 10 women to every man, so that cuts down my possibilities of finding a partner around my age range. I am seriously thinking about either major surgery on my face or something that will be coming up in the near future that would be an anti-aging procedure.

Thus, in order to increase her social currency and ability to garner a more privileged position in the dating scene, the woman was willing to undergo extensive surgical intervention. Also concerned that her relationship with her younger partner was fragile and insecure, a 60-year-old, middle-class woman asserted that she felt compelled to work on her appearance in order to retain his attention:

> I do feel pressure to look younger. My boyfriend is younger than me and I wouldn't want to get too old looking because of the age difference between us. He's 53, and I'm 60. I think he could be dating someone who is 40 quite easily. So there's pressure on me to look good. Or I feel that pressure anyway. I guess because too, I really don't have a real commitment from him, either. It's a different world out there when you're single, and I'm lonely. . . . I don't think I'd be quite this frivolous if I was still married. I would be travelling in different circles. I'd be at the church supper every Sunday night. . . . I'd be a little more relaxed about my appearance.

Even those who were happily married did not feel immune to the demands to engage in beauty work so as to maintain their sexual currency and the attention of their partners. For example, a 65-year-old, upper-class woman who had used hair dye, makeup, and Botox and Restylane injections stated:

> I became worried about my appearance in that I felt that if a younger woman came into the picture—not that he has lady friends, but you know, I just felt a little bit threatened somehow. I began feeling a little bit threatened by other women . . . and I think that's why I probably started becoming more aware of my appearance.

Consequently, the actual or feared loss of male attention amplified the women's receptiveness to anti-aging discourses and their enthusiasm for the disciplining of their bodies.

Additionally, the work world was identified as a contentious place for many aging women. For example, the women who were in the process of changing careers or trying to find employment made comments similar to those of a 61-year-old, divorced woman who had an undergraduate degree and a middle-class income and who had had laser facial resurfacing:

> I don't want injections. I don't want radical surgery at this point. But I work with the public so I want to look younger. . . . I've been to many, many interviews. You know, I'm 61. And in my type of work, they want younger people. So I had laser treatments done. . . . Now I'm considering going for a peel for my wrinkles.

As well as competing for jobs, women who worked with the public stated that they felt pressured to retain a youthful appearance in order to be successful in the health- and image-oriented industries. In this way, the women used or were contemplating using non-surgical cosmetic procedures to avoid the age stereotyping that has been shown to be particularly oppressive to women in the workplace (Duncan & Loretto, 2004; Itzin & Phillipson, 1993; Itzin & Phillipson, 1995; Walker et al., 2007). A married, 51-year-old, upper-class woman who had had microdermabrasion stated the following:

> I think at work there is pressure to look younger. . . . Just being a health care worker, I think you have to practice what you preach. . . . Appearance is very important I think. At work you try and look smart because we're representing an image and we're trying to teach patients . . . so appearance is important for you to value.

Collectively, the women commented on the increasing devaluation of being and looking older. For example, a 62-year-old woman who had a very limited income argued:

> Nowadays it's nothing like what it was years ago. Nothing. Before, growing old, it was, well it was a natural thing to do. But now everybody, like I said, these people are pushing, "Why would you look your age? We can stop you from looking like an old hag! Buy some of our junk." Um, I don't know. And I guess too because the divorce rate is so high now,

and women and men alike are falling for this crap, thinking it's going to help them out in their next marriage or relationship or whatever. They're gonna need a whole bucket of Botox!

Some women asserted that women were at particular social risk as a result of aging and oppressive discourses of ageism. For example, a 65-year-old, middle-class woman stated:

Our attitude toward older people, particularly older women, is that they've lost their power and they're insignificant and, taken to an extreme, they're of no value anymore. They're a drain on the tax dollar. That's a strong message there. And we do it to older women—older people. We put them in old age homes and lump them all together. It's the cruellest, cruellest thing we can do to older people. It's just a terrible thing!

Consequently, some women expressed trepidation about the future as they commented on the image of losing their social currency as a result of their changing physical appearances. A 65-year-old, middle-class woman contended:

I wish I could say that I feel at peace about ageing and that I will let things play out the way they do. But if I gave you an honest answer today, I think I'm scared because I know that essentially the world thinks old things and old people are kind of like garbage. I'm just holding my own and when I look like a piece of garbage, it's probably how I'll be treated.

Regardless of their responses to anti-aging discourses, many women also worried about the impact that current beauty standards, marketing practices, and media messages would have on younger and future generations of women. A 71-year-old, middle-class woman who had used microdermabrasion in the past reflected: "If I succumb to it—and I'm kind of on the fringe or marginal given my age and status—then how much more are younger women or middle-aged women going to be affected? You can't escape this!" In other words, the woman felt that because of her age and life experience she was more protected from or at least less susceptible to the persuasiveness of the anti-aging messages and the resultant assault on her self-esteem. She and some of the other women suggested that their younger female counterparts lacked the wisdom and clarity to see through the false marketing, the misguided societal emphasis on appearance, or the unrealistic nature of the current beauty ideal. A 56-year-old woman who had an undeclared income expressed the following concerns:

> My idea of the ideal female body is one that has curves. One that looks female as opposed to male or like Pat, where you can't tell what Pat is, you know? I guess I still like to see the femininity and . . . the glow of the personality of the person inside. That's where the beauty is—the beauty isn't in the vessel. It's the twinkle in the eye, it's the giggle. That's what makes the beauty of the person, not their $5,000 boobs and their $500 nose job. You know, and I'm sad to say that a lot of our youth are really being led down the garden path through all this marketing and that's because the emphasis is so much on the packaging and not what is in the package.

Even as the women stressed the importance of personality and personal character over the external façade of the individual, their own internalization of extant ageist discourses rendered their perception that they were less at risk than younger women suspect. Nevertheless, the women suggested that the escalating bombardment of media images of beauty and the growing availability of beauty products and services made the navigation of doing gender in an ageist world increasingly difficult and socially hazardous. A woman, who was 64 years old and had a middle-class income, stated:

> You see a lot of young women doing all this stuff like tanning salons and other things, which is a little scary. So, the media has definitely got a huge influence. And I think it definitely has a way greater impact on the younger age group . . . like I'm just thinking of my granddaughters. They have more makeup than I would ever have dreamed of having in my whole life. Yeah. Kits of the stuff. They go through the whole thing.

Given that the younger women did not have the same historical access to curvier female actresses such as Marilyn Monroe as reference points as well as the proliferation of advertising via television, the Internet, magazines, and movies, the women worried that the younger women were at much greater risk of developing eating disorders and negative body images. For example, a 55-year-old, upper-class woman had this to say:

> The effect the media has on these girls and their self-esteem . . . and the damage they do to their bodies . . . it really strikes a nerve with me. I get very angry at times when I think of the media and I think of the air brushing that they do in these magazines. . . . I think that it's the disem-powerment of the girls, the young girls seeing these things. Kids at 12 really don't have a sense of identity yet . . . it's difficult to take sometimes.

In this way, the women articulated a strong fear that their daughters and granddaughters would buy into the digitally constructed and enhanced ideals of beauty that were humanly impossible to achieve to the detriment of their own self-esteem. While they themselves had largely embraced these ideals, the women seemed to hope for a better future for the generations of women to come.

## SUMMARY AND CONCLUSIONS

Reflecting and amplifying ageist ideologies that permeate Western culture, advertising is one of the most powerful ways by which the face of aging is constructed and reinforced. While the extant research has established that ageism has long been prevalent in movies, print advertisements, television programming, and other media contexts, the rise of what has come to be known as anti-aging consumer culture has magnified these discourses. This intensification has coincided with population aging and has occurred by virtue of the increased marketing of products and services designed to stop or reverse the aging process, as well as through the explicit denigration of and antipathy toward aged bodies. Indeed, the age relations underscoring this phenomenon are not modestly couched in politically correct language, as we are rather proudly and openly hostile toward or "anti" aging.

The unequivocal vilification of aging generally and aged appearances in particular is especially evident in beauty product advertisements. While the products vary in their aims and scope, they collectively and strongly assert the need to battle destiny and make appropriate anti-aging beauty work choices in order to retain one's social value. Individuals are bombarded with the message that youthfulness is a commodity that is simultaneously easy to acquire, vital to one's social visibility and subsequent cultural worth, and detachable from and, therefore, not limited by one's chronological age. To that end, beauty advertisements are rooted in extant societal binaries of young versus old, beautiful versus ugly, visible versus invisible, smooth versus wrinkled, luminous versus dull, healthy versus sick, and sexually attractive versus sexually unappealing.

At the same time, anti-aging discourses embedded in beauty advertisements mirror healthism (Crawford, 1980), as they construct aging as a deviant, if not diseased, state and promulgate the assumption that the individual has a moral responsibility to fight the onset of an aged appearance. Calasanti (2007, p. 342) aptly states: "The message is not merely that one can control aging . . . the point is that individuals *should* control aging." Moreover, the act of controlling one's age, specifically the appearance of age, is framed as a battleground of commercialism versus destiny. The language of aggression permeates the advertisements as youthfulness is held up as heroic victor or prized fighter while agedness is beaten down into submission and given its *good* rightful place at the bottom of the social hierarchy.

While the language that is openly hostile toward the aged body is readily apparent, one of the more sly and insidious aspects of anti-aging beauty advertisements is the use of pseudoscientific language to justify and legitimate the product claims. As well as proclaiming that they represent important, novel, even revolutionary breakthroughs, many of the products mimic the names of non-surgical cosmetic procedures (e.g., Botox, hyaluronic acid, and Restylane). Such clever and subtle impersonations serve to transform over-the-counter, garden-variety creams into extraordinary, if not magical, formulas with the potential to erase or halt the ravages of aging. Additionally, the endorsements suggest that the products are safer, more natural, more effective, and/or less expensive than surgery, injections, microdermabrasion, or laser treatments. In this way, the products claim to have the benefits of the more expensive, intrusive non-surgical cosmetic procedures without the risks, and thereby further extend the notion that non-surgical anti-aging beauty work treatments and products are accessible to all. Regardless of the nature of the marketing strategies and slogans employed by the advertisements, the underlying message is resoundingly clear and oppressive: To look old is to be found morally, socially, and aesthetically wanting, and failure to even try to fight the appearance of aging is wholly unacceptable.

Older women's responses to these advertisements and other media messages are complex, ambivalent, and contradictory. On one hand, the women rejected the models used in the photographs as well as those who appeared on fashion runways because of their tendency to be gaunt rather than curvy, as they advocated adherence to a Marilyn Monroe figure over a Twiggy-like shape. The women emphasized the importance of having voluptuous figures in order to achieve idealized beauty and femininity. However, the women's stated preference for curvier bodies stood in stark contrast to their own dissatisfaction with their weight and their possession of more shapely bodies, as was discussed in chapter 4.

Although the women largely embraced the broader societal emphasis on youthfulness as a crucial component of physical attractiveness, they described feeling bombarded and angered by ageist media messages that deemed their own appearances to have become increasingly divergent from extant notions of feminine beauty. The advertisements in particular highlighted and exploited the exclusion the women experienced in their interactions with younger individuals as well as with potential romantic partners. Combined with the pressures the women experienced in the workplace to look younger and, therefore, attractive and healthy, the women's perceived inadequacies in their relationships with younger individuals and especially men lead them to feel a profound sense of urgency to attend to their appearances so as to remain visible, credible, competitive, and valued. In this way, the women expressed poignant internal tensions between struggling with the realities of ageism in their everyday lives, feeling compelled to engage in beauty work in order to be socially acceptable and relevant, and balking at the societal demeaning of aged bodies and appearances. Even as they expressed awareness of the artificiality of the advertisements and the manipulative nature of the slogans and images, the women also frequently indicated that they were knowingly "sucked in" by the promises of various beauty products because of their awareness of the importance of looking younger. In this way, the need to be beautiful, feminine, and socially acceptable trumped rational assessments of the insidious impact of ageist discourses and fears about the social and physical realition of growing older.

That said, there were a few women who suggested that they were impervious to the influence of anti-aging discourses in the media. These women contended that appearance had never been a focus in their lives, although they struggled to identify reasons for their distance from, if not resistance to, beauty culture. While some suggested that they did not derive pleasure from doing beauty, others articulated a reevaluation of priorities over time, whereby the emphasis on appearance when they were younger and seeking out male attention had been replaced by a concern for health, physical fitness, and long-term relationships. Undoubtedly, these women stood in stark contrast to the more common pattern, whereby the women I spoke with usually described having had a lifelong concern for appearance and beauty work, with a concomitant threat to their sense of self-esteem, security in relationships, and identity as their bodies increasingly deviated from idealized beauty standards. Having never stood outside of beauty culture and by virtue of their predominantly White, heterosexual, middle- and upper-middle-class affiliation, as well as their strong investment in appearance, the women's privilege in society made them more susceptible to the impact of ageism on their sense of well-being and feminine identities.

The women's responses to older movie stars underscored further contradictions in their attitudes toward female bodies and beauty work in later life. The women were simultaneously harsh and begrudgingly complimentary in their assessments of the appearances of aging film stars currently in the media. Individuals such as Helen Mirren and Meryl Streep were held up as exemplars of aging well, although their wrinkles and other visible signs of aging were identified as disappointing and unattractive flaws. Other film stars such as Susan Sarandon, who had become a spokesperson for Revlon's Age-Defying Makeup, were repeatedly described as having lost their credibility because of their apparent embracement of anti-aging technology, be that through the personal use of cosmetic surgery or their endorsement of anti-aging products. Clearly, if even the world's most beautiful women are considered flawed and disappointing or disingenuous by virtue of their attempts to mitigate their perceived appearance inadequacies, the implications and realities of physical aging for the average older woman are truly devastating. Indeed, to age naturally is to be found wanting, while the use of anti-aging beauty technologies renders the individual fraudulent and, therefore, also imperfect (Hurd Clarke & Griffin, 2007a). In this way, the doing of gender (West & Zimmerman, 1987) successfully through the achievement of idealized beauty in later life becomes an impossible mission as older women are condemned and found inadequate no matter what beauty work choices they make.

Interestingly, the women tended to be most concerned about the impact of the media and idealized beauty standards on the younger generations rather than on themselves. Thus, although they acknowledged that they themselves were being strongly influenced by societal ageist discourses and images, they suggested that it was younger women who were most at risk of social and emotional consequences such as loss of self-esteem or even the development of eating disorders because of their inability to achieve and maintain ideal feminine beauty. In this way, the women simultaneously constructed themselves as being both impervious to negative media messages and the victims of ageist discourses. Establishing younger women as the "other" who was the ultimate target of negative media messages buttressed their own social and emotional security through the perception that they were able to rise above insidiously ageist marketing campaigns. However, even as they argued that their own life experiences and ages afforded them wisdom and cultural capital to resist the undermining of their self-esteem via the ubiquity of ageist ideologies, the women's use of distancing tactics to suggest that ageism was external to their daily realities was belied by their own internalization of and adherence to these discriminatory values and practices. Indeed, the women's overarching dissatisfaction with their bodies muted and contradicted their assertions that they were somehow immune to ageist beauty standards.

# 6

❧

# Women and Aging:
# The Face of the Future

Decline is a metaphor as hard to contain as dye. Once it has tinged our expectations of the future (sensations, rewards, status, power, voice) with peril, it tends to stain our experiences, our views of others, our explanatory systems, and then our retrospective judgements. (Gullette, 2004, p. 11)

In the preceding chapters I examined the complexities of women's experiences and perceptions of aging and their changing bodies within anti-aging culture. Although older women's body image is elastic and situational (Myers & Biocca, 1992; Paquette & Raine, 2004), their feelings in and about their bodies are strongly influenced by ageist discourses that narrowly define beauty in terms of the possession of youthfulness (Calasanti & Slevin, 2001; Cruikshank, 2003; Furman, 1997; Holstein, 2006; Hurd, 1999; Wolf, 1991). Similar to their younger counterparts, older women are normatively discontented (Rodin et al., 1985) with their bodies. However, as well as targeting their weights as a source of dissatisfaction in ways similar to younger women, older women convey strong displeasure with their gray hair, wrinkles, and sagging flesh. Thus, older women's pejorative and often self-loathing appearance evaluations are rooted in their perceptions of "age as an enemy" (Seid, 1989, p. 17) that has progressively robbed them of their youthfulness and, therefore, of an essential source of cultural capital.

Older women's dissatisfaction with their appearances is undoubt-edly reinforced by aesthetic medicine, by pharmaceutical and cosmet-ics companies, and by the media. Indeed, physicians and corporations are the ultimate winners in the age relations that underlie beauty ideology, which dictates that women are never good enough and that the need for beauty work never ends (Bartky, 1998; Bordo, 2003). The power of these groups can be seen in the shifts in the emergent ways that women view their wrinkles. Prior to the development of non-surgical cosmetic procedures, the women I interviewed were evenly split in their positive and negative interpretations of facial creases. Fol-lowing the emergence of non-surgical cosmetic procedures, I noticed an increased negativity toward wrinkles as well as the use of new language to describe particular facial creases. Specifically, women learned that certain wrinkles were especially loathsome and in need of medical and cosmetic remediation. Wrinkles that could be treated with Botox injections and injectable fillers were described as ugly and as having negative emotions attached to and embedded in them. In contrast, wrinkles for which no medical intervention currently existed were depicted in relatively benign ways. In this way, women's atti-tudes toward their wrinkles corresponded with the current bounds of medicine and the pharmaceutical and cosmetic companies' advertis-ing campaigns, thereby demonstrating the power of beauty ideology to influence individuals' feelings about and experiences in their aging bodies.

The construction of age as an adversary that can and must be fought is built upon the uncritical—and, indeed, often unrecognized—acceptance of the deeply entrenched societal veneration and privileg-ing of youthfulness as "naturally" better. Older women argue that the equation of youthfulness with beauty is an irrefutable fact of nature. These views are reinforced by the medicalization of beauty and the rise of aesthetic and anti-aging medicine, which collectively aim to eradicate aging and oldness. The notion of beauty being physically determined and situated is further underscored by the double stan-dard of aging and by physicians who contend that men are superior biologically (for example, the assertion that men's skin is thicker and more resistant to wrinkles) and, therefore, do not have to work as hard at maintaining, if not enhancing, their appearances. Therefore, loss of physical attractiveness over time is perceived and experienced as an inevitable, biological truth rather than one that is socially embedded and culturally constructed.

Despite the societal assumption that declining beauty is biologically situated, it is through social interaction that older women learn how to see their aging bodies and how to respond to the onset of the visible signs of aging. Women learn what is culturally valued and privileged from their peers and female significant others (Hurd Clarke & Griffin, 2007a) as well as in the context of the workplace and romantic relationships (Hurd Clarke & Griffin, 2008a). Specifically, the men and women with whom women interact on a daily basis teach them that youthfulness is attractive, sexy, healthy, and normative while agedness is equated with ugliness, asexuality, loss of health, and deviance. Taught to rigorously and unflinchingly scrutinize their own appearances and the appearances of others, women become adept at identifying and scorning those who fail to measure up. Consequently, the doing of gender, age, and beauty (West & Zimmerman, 1987) are relational processes that are embedded in a social context and shaped by relentless and unforgiving ageist and sexist (not to mention racist, classist, and heteronormative) ideologies.

Women experience their inevitable loss of youthful appearances in a range of ways. For some, declining physical attractiveness is met with dismay, sadness, and disgruntlement (Hurd, 2000). Notably, it is the loss of a slim, svelte figure that is the source of particular self-recrimination as women often express a strong sense of culpability about their increased weights and concomitant loss of perceived attractiveness. Thus, women's appearance evaluations are strongly influenced by healthist discourses that hold individuals personally responsible for the health and appearance (which are assumed to be one and the same thing) of their bodies (Crawford, 1980; Oberg & Tornstam, 2001; White et al., 1995). The gradual loss of good looks that accompanies aging leads to a painful dissonance and to assaults on the self-esteem of many women as their external facades and reflected images contradict their perceptions of themselves as youthful individuals.

Still other women suggest that appearances are trivial and that what truly matters is health and functional abilities (Hurd, 2000). Faced with declining health, the potential future loss of independence as well as a declining ability to successfully engage in beauty culture, these women are painfully aware that physical breakdown will culminate in the most profound form of social exclusion. Not only will the women experience disparagement of their appearances, they may also be faced with dependence on others for their personal care and even segregation and social isolation. Nevertheless, the women rarely dwell on their fears of aging and dying, preferring to frame their lives positively and with gratitude for all of their remaining social and physical abilities and resources. By recasting the importance of their appearances and comparing their own bodies to their less fortunate peers, the women preserve a meaningful and affirmative sense of identity and well-being.

Finally, some women struggle to reconcile their dissatisfaction with their aging bodies and faces with their personal values that either disparage vanity or reject sexist discourses. These women describe an ongoing vacillation between self-acceptance and disappointment with bodies that have become more wrinkled, have gained weight, or have begun to appear more aged. Similarly, these women express uneasiness about their own engagement with or disengagement from beauty culture as a result of the ideological underpinnings of feminine beauty requirements and the social perils of appearing old.

At the same time, the medicalization of appearance has redefined what is old and what is not. Indeed, anti-aging and ageist ideologies suggest that youthfulness is a quality that is not limited by chronological age, and, therefore, by biology. Rather, there is a presumed difference between looking old or young and being old or young such that one's felt age is either masked by or revealed by one's appearance (Holstein, 2001, 2006; Hurd, 1999; Hurd Clarke, 2001). In other words, an individual can feel young "on the inside" irrespective of their chronological age or appearance. Feeling young is signalled by a sense of energy, vibrancy, and social engagement, while feeling old is equated with negative stereotypes that warrant and result in social exclusion (Hurd, 1999; Katz, 2001). Depending on one's willingness and ability to engage in physically transforming and intrusive beauty work, an individual can achieve greater (though not necessarily exact) parity between her appearance and her felt age and corresponding felt identity. Consequently, women are faced with strong pressure to resist through conformity (Holstein, 2001, 2006), by using all available means to not look their age. Appearance is a battleground on which cultural capital is won and lost, and beauty work is a deeply political and often unconscious and taken-for-granted act that is circumscribed and required by ageist and sexist ideologies. The ever-increasing numbers of beauty products and services available to women to assist in their quest to hang on to their youthful appearances for as long as possible serves to bolster the belief that not only can one fight the ravages of time, but that one is also morally obligated to do so. The ultimately doomed fight against aging is both physical and moral, as individuals embrace healthist discourses that assign social currency to physical exteriors. Against the backdrop of perceptions of ethical responsibility, individuals who look old and, therefore, ugly and unhealthy—by virtue of their hair color, wrinkled skin, altered body shapes, or increased weight—are presumed to have morally, socially, and physically failed in their clash with the never-ending advancement of time.

Not only are individuals presumed to have been vanquished in their battle with age when they begin to look old, they are also rendered socially and sometimes even physically invisible (Holstein, 2001) to others. Older women convey the sense that they lose their personhood, ability to socially engage with others, and rights of citizenship when interacting with younger individuals or men who are taught to seek out and value youthfulness in their sexual partners. Whether they are walked into while proceeding down the sidewalk by seemingly oblivious younger individuals or completely ignored and discounted by their male peers and potential mates, the women describe a descent into social oblivion and a loss of social privilege that solely derives from their changing physical exteriors. Changing appearances and the concomitant failure to age successfully become the means by which individuals are socially excluded and disparaged. In other words, aged appearances are not only equated with negative stereotypes, they are also the most immediate, if not important, way that older adults are identified, set apart, denied opportunities and social currency, and thereby oppressed.

Nevertheless, striving to be visible by applying cosmetics, dyeing one's hair, purchasing injections, or even going under the knife is not enough. The product of beauty work should appear undetectable and, therefore, passable as natural (Hurd Clarke & Griffin, 2007a). While the natural or unadorned female body is considered to be unacceptable and lacking in femininity, the body that has been obviously altered is disingenuous and equally unacceptable. Women are forced to run a gauntlet of scrutiny whereby their work on and attention to their appearances are seen to walk the fine, if not impossible, line between doing too much and not doing enough. An individual who fails to dye her gray hair is considered unattractive, while an older woman whose hair is obviously dyed or colored in what is perceived to be an inappropriate color is subject to castigation as being inauthentic, if not ridiculous. Similarly, aging movie stars whose faces are now lined with wrinkles are considered flawed and less beautiful, while those actresses whose faces attest to cosmetic surgery gone wrong and/ or non-surgical cosmetic procedures that are obviously apparent are hostilely derided.

Of course, there has been much debate in the feminist literature about whether beauty work is creative, pleasurable, empowering, and liberating (Beausoleil, 1994; Davis, 1997; Gimlin, 2000; Negrin, 2002; Weitz, 2001) or whether it is form of sexual oppression that serves to keep women docile and insecure (Bartky, 1998; Bordo, 2003; Hesse-Biber, 1996; Seid, 1994). While there is no question that women are taught to revel in and derive pleasure from fashion and cosmetics and other forms of doing gender through the body, or that achieving a closer approximation to idealized beauty can enhance one's social power and opportunities, anti-aging discourses and the fight to preserve a youthful appearance starkly belie the supposedly benign nature of engaging in beauty regimens. Clearly, older women are compelled to engage in beauty work, irrespective of the futility of their efforts, or face social eradication because of the societal definition of beauty and the power attributed to culturally valued appearances, for as one physician put it, "youth rule the world."

While the majority of women I have interviewed have engaged in some form of beauty work, including dieting, the use of cosmetics or hair dye, non-surgical cosmetic procedures, and/or cosmetic surgery, the ways in which women describe beauty work and their reasons for attending to their appearances reveal the complex and subtle ways delv ded

that sexism and ageism are internalized and embraced. For example, older women often deny their own internalized ageism by suggesting that their disavowal of gray hair has to do with personal taste or suitability rather than stemming from a disparagement of oldness. Similarly, some women who use cosmetics, hair dye, cosmetic surgery, or non-surgical cosmetic procedures contest the idea that they are socially pressured to attend to their appearances and argue that their efforts stem from the personal pleasure that they derive from the beauty practices. The pain of some of these beauty practices notwithstanding, it is clear that the pleasure that the women experience ultimately derives from the achievement of a culturally valued appearance, and, therefore, from their acceptance of ageist and sexist discourses that define women's value in relation to their appearance and that equate beauty with youthfulness.

Finally, the relationship between social position and beauty ideology warrants further comment. As discussed in chapter 2, definitions of idealized beauty and levels of body image dissatisfaction are shaped by age, class, ethnicity, and sexual orientation. Similarly, Holstein (2001) has pointed out that an older woman's ability to engage in beauty culture is limited by her access to resources. The majority of women that I have spoken with have been White, heterosexual, and middle class, and thus my ability to speak to the influence of social position is limited. Future research that investigates the beauty practices of diverse older women with particular attention to ethnicity, sexual preference, and social class are needed. That said, my data highlight the powerful influence of ageist discourses on women's experiences of growing older in an image-obsessed and anti-aging culture. While the women have uncritically accepted ageist conceptualizations of beauty, they have also expressed a preference for more curvaceous bodies than are typically identified by their younger counterparts or are visible in the media (Hurd Clarke, 2002a; Lamb et al., 1993). From Marilyn Monroe to Queen Latifah, the women suggest that figures that are shapelier than those embodied by Twiggy or Paris Hilton are ones that they esteem and aspire to emulate. Notably, the women's endorsement of curvier bodies is juxtaposed against and contradicted by their disparagement of their own heavier bodies and their identification of their weight gains as a particularly abhorrent form of moral failure. Nevertheless, the women contend that the extremes of thinness embodied in contemporary beauty ideals are potentially devastating for the younger generations of women who have not been exposed to alternative, curvier definitions of beauty, who perhaps lack the wisdom and experience to see through the persuasively deceptive media images and who face an increasing commodification and medicalization of beauty.

## CONCLUSION

It is clear that aging, feelings about appearances, and decisions about beauty work are deeply personal, intensely political, and fraught with contradictions. In my own daily life and my journey through this research, I struggle to reconcile my intellectual grasp and inherent critique of beauty work with my personal choices (such as my own use of hair dye), my influence over my children (my daughter in particular), and my future expectations about growing older. Reflecting on the futures of my grandmothers, my mother, and my daughter, as well as on my privileged opportunities to have spoken with so many older women over the years about their experiences of growing older, has solidified in me the need to continue to fight ageism. Thus, I often reflect on Furman's (1997) call for resistance of age-based discrimination and exclusion so that "women may begin to reclaim their right to age without stigma" (Arber & Ginn, 1991a, p. 49).

As long as appearance concerns are taken for granted or deemed trivial, the powerful ageist and sexist agendas underlying them are accepted and reinforced. Although conformity to extant gendered beauty norms means that we achieve certain social ends, in the long term we write our own eventual descent into social oblivion (Holstein, 2006). The face of aging will inevitably continue to grow younger as aesthetic medicine's boundaries expand; new aspects of the aging face and body are mined for aesthetic intervention; the scope of ageist appearance norms expand to encompass and attack all citizens regardless of age, gender, class, ethnicity, or sexual preference; appearances increasingly become the barometer of peoples' health, social currency, and morality; and individuals in society continue to embrace gendered ageism to their own ultimate detriment. Older women, like their younger and male counterparts, will face increasing pressure to further alter and discipline their bodies or risk losing social visibility, access to employment and partners, and the respect of the younger generations. In this way, the increasing attention to appearance and the concomitant "new form of ageism" (Holstein, 2001) will become further entrenched and more insidious.

My hope is that by making the taken-for-granted assumptions about older women and their appearances more evident and examining the complexities of women's feelings about their bodies and aging, we may consider ways of living and aging differently. To see older women and their current social devaluation as somehow separate from ourselves, irrespective of our gender, age, or investment in appearance, is to lose our humanity.

good

But all her attention.

intensalized Ageism,

somewhat de humanizing

# References

Abell, S. C., & Richards, M. H. (1996). The relationship between body shape satisfaction and self-esteem: An investigation of gender and class differences. *Journal of Youth and Adolescence, 25* (5), 691–703.

Adams, A., Buckingham, C. D., Arber, S., McKinlay, J. B., Marceau, L., & Link, C. (2006). The influence of patient's age on clinical decision-making about coronary heart disease in the USA and the UK. *Ageing and Society, 26* (2), 303–21.

Akan, G. E., & Grilo, C. M. (1995). Sociocultural influences on eating attitudes and behaviors, body image, and psychological functioning: A comparison of African-American, Asian-American, and Caucasian college women. *International Journal of Eating Disorders, 18* (2), 181–87.

Allaz, A. F., Bernstein, M., Rouget, P., Archinard, M., & Morabia, A. (1998). Body weight preoccupation in middle-age and ageing women: A general population survey. *International Journal of Eating Disorders, 23* (3), 287–94.

Allergan. Earnings releases. Last retrieved from http://agn360.client.shareholder.com/earnings.cfm on November 1, 2008.

Altabe, M. (1998). Ethnicity and body image: Quantitative and qualitative analysis. *International Journal of Eating Disorders, 23* (2), 153–59.

American Academy of Anti-Aging Medicine (A4M). (n.d.). Last retrieved from www.worldhealth.net on September 18, 2008.

American Society for Aesthetic Plastic Surgery. (2010). Last retrieved from www.surgery.org/sites/default/files/2009stats.pdf on April 20, 2010.

American Society of Plastic Surgeons. (2009). 2000/2007/2008 National plastic surgery statistics: Cosmetic and reconstructive procedure trends. Last retrieved from www.plasticsurgery.org/Media/stats/2008-cosmetic-reconstructive-plastic-surgery-minimally-invasive-statistics.pdf on April 20, 2010.

Arber, S., & Ginn, J. (1991a). *Gender and later life: A sociological analysis of resources and constraints*. London: Sage.

Arber, S., & Ginn, J. (1991b). The invisibility of age: Gender and class in later life. *Sociological Review, 39* (2), 268–91.

Baker, L., & Gringart, E. (2009). Body image and self-esteem in older adulthood. *Ageing and Society, 29* (6), 977–95.

Ballard, K. D., Elston, M. A., & Gabe, J. (2009). Private and public ageing in the UK: The transition through the menopause. *Current Sociology, 57* (2), 269–90.

Banks, I. (2000). *Hair matters: Beauty, power, and black women's consciousness*. New York: New York University Press.

Barnett, R. C. (2005). Ageism and sexism in the workplace. *Generations, 29* (3), 25–30.

Bartky, S. L. (1998). Foucault, femininity, and the modernization of patriarchal power. In R. Weitz (Ed.), *The politics of women's bodies: Sexuality, appearance, and behavior* (pp. 25–45). New York: Oxford University Press.

Bazzini, D. G., McIntosh, W. D., Smith, S. M., Cook, S., and Harris, C. (1997). The aging woman in popular film: Underrepresented, unattractive, unfriendly, and unintelligent. *Sex Roles, 36* (7/8), 531–43.

Beausoleil, N. (1994). Makeup in everyday life: An inquiry into the practices of urban American women of diverse backgrounds. In N. Sault (Ed.), *Many mirrors: Body image and social relations* (pp. 33–57). New Brunswick, NJ: Rutgers University Press.

Becker, G., & Kaufman, S. R. (1995). Managing an uncertain illness trajectory in old age: Patients' and physicians' views of stroke. *Medical Anthropology Quarterly, 9* (2), 165–87.

Bedford, J. L., & Johnson, C. S. (2005). Societal influences on body image dissatisfaction in younger and older women. *Journal of Women and Aging, 18* (1), 41–55.

Bendick, M., Jackson, C. W., & Romero, J. H. (1996). Employment discrimination against older workers: An experimental study of hiring practices. *Journal of Aging and Social Policy, 8* (4), 25–46.

Beren, S. E., Hayden, H. A., Wilfley, D. E., & Grilo, C. M. (1996). The influence of sexual orientation on body dissatisfaction in adult men and women. *International Journal of Eating Disorders, 20* (2), 135–41.

Berger, E. D. (2006). "Aging" identities: Degradation and negotiation in the search for employment. *Journal of Aging Studies, 20* (4), 303–16.

Bergeron, S. M., & Senn, C. Y. (1998). Body image and sociocultural norms: A comparison of heterosexual and lesbian women. *Psychology of Women Quarterly, 22* (3), 385–401.

Binstock, R. H., Fishman, J. R., & Johnson, T. E, (2006). Anti-aging medicine and science: Social implications. In R. H. Binstock & L. K. George (Eds.), *Handbook of aging and the social sciences* (6th ed.) (pp. 436–55). Burlington, MA: Academic Press.

Black, P., & Sharma, U. (2001). Men are real, women are "made up": Beauty therapy and the construction of femininity. *The Sociological Review, 49* (1), 100–116.

Blood, S. K. (2005). *Body work: The social construction of women's body image.* New York: Routledge.

Bordo, S. (2003). *Unbearable weight: Feminism, Western culture and the body* (10th anniversary ed.). Los Angeles: University of California Press.

Bordo, S. (2009). Twenty years in the twilight zone. In C. J. Heyes and M. Jones (Eds.), *Cosmetic surgery: A feminist primer* (pp. 21–33). Burlington, VT: Ashgate.

Boughton, M. A. (2002). Premature menopause: Multiple disruptions between the woman's biological body experience and her lived body. *Journal of Advanced Nursing, 37* (5), 423–30.

Bowd, A. D. (2003). Stereotypes of elderly persons in narrative jokes. *Research on Aging, 25* (1), 22–35.

Brand, P. A., Rothblum, E. D., & Solomon, L. J. (1992). A comparison of lesbians, gay men, and heterosexuals on weight and restrained eating. *International Journal of Eating Disorders, 11* (3), 253–59.

Brooks, A. T. (2010). Aesthetic anti-ageing surgery and technology: Women's friend or foe? *Sociology of Health and Illness, 32* (2), 238–57.

Brown, C., & Jasper, K. (1993). Introduction: Why weight? Why women? Why now? In C. Brown & K. Jasper (Eds.), *Consuming passions: Feminist approaches to weight preoccupation and eating disorders* (pp. 16–35). Toronto: Second Story.

Brown, L. S. (1987). Lesbians, weight and eating: New analyses and perspectives. In the Boston Lesbian Psychologies Collective (Eds.), *Lesbian psychologies: Explorations and challenges* (pp. 294–309). Chicago: University of Illinois Press.

Bury, M. (1982). Chronic illness as biographical disruption. *Sociology of Health and Illness, 4* (2), 167–82.

Bury, M. (1988). Meanings at risk: The experience of arthritis. In R. Anderson & M. Bury (Eds.), *Living with chronic illness: The experience of patients and their families* (pp. 89–116). London: Unwin Hyman.

Butler, J. (1990). *Gender trouble: Feminism and the subversion of identity.* New York: Routledge.

Butler, R. (1969). Ageism: Another form of bigotry. *The Gerontologist, 9* (3), 243–46.

Butler, R. (1980). Ageism: A foreword. *Journal of Social Issues, 36* (2), 8–11.

Bytheway, B. (1995). *Ageism.* Philadelphia: Open University Press.

Cachelin, F. M., Rebeck, R. M., Chung, G. H., & Pelayo, E. (2002). Does ethnicity influence body-size preference? A comparison of body image and body size. *Obesity Research, 10* (3), 158–66.

Calasanti, T. (2005). Ageism, gravity, and gender: Experiences of aging bodies. *Generations, 29* (3), 8–12.

Calasanti, T. (2007). Bodacious berry, potency wood and the aging monster: Gender and age relations in anti-aging ads. *Social Forces, 86* (1), 335–55.

Calasanti, T. M., & Slevin, K. (2001). *Gender, social inequalities, and aging.* New York: AltaMira Press.

Canales, M. K. (2000). Othering: Toward an understanding of difference. *Advances in Nursing Science, 22* (4), 16–31.

Carpenter, L. M., Nathanson, C. A., & Kim, Y. J. (2006). Physical women, emotional men: Gender and sexual satisfaction in midlife. *Archives of Sexual Behavior, 38* (1), 87–107.

Carrigan, M., & Szmigin, I. (2000). Advertising in an ageing society. *Ageing and Society, 20* (2), 217–33.

Cash, T. F., Ancis, J. R., & Strachan, M. D. (1997). Gender attitudes, feminist identity, and body images among college women. *Sex Roles, 36* (7/8), 433–47.

Cash, T. F., & Henry, P. E. (1995). Women's body images: The results of a national survey in the U.S.A. *Sex Roles, 33* (1/2), 19–28.

Cash, T. F., Morrow, J. A., Hrabosky, J. I., & Perry, A. A. (2004). How has body image changed? A cross-sectional investigation of college women and men from 1983 to 2001. *Journal of Consulting and Clinical Psychology, 72* (6), 1081–89.

Cepanec, D., & Payne, B. (2000). "Old bags" under the knife: Facial cosmetic surgery among women. In B. Miedema, J. M. Stoppard, & V. Anderson (Eds.), *Women bodies: Women's lives* (pp. 121–41). Toronto: Sumach.

Charmaz, K. (1995). The body, identity, and self: Adapting to impairment. *The Sociological Quarterly, 36* (4), 657–80.

Chiu, W. C. K., Chan, A. W., Snape, E., & Redman, T. (2001). Age stereotypes and discriminatory attitudes towards older workers: An East-West comparison. *Human Relations, 54* (5), 629–61.

Chrisler, J. C., & Ghiz, L. (1993). Body image issues of older women. In N. D. Davis, E. Cole, & E. D. Rothblum (Eds.), *Faces of women and aging* (pp. 67–75). New York: Harrington Park.

Cogan, J. C. (1999). Lesbians walk the tightrope of beauty: Thin is in but femme is out. *Journal of Lesbian Studies, 3* (4), 77–89.

Connidis, I. (2006). Intimate relationships: Learning from later life experience. In T. M. Calasanti & K. F. Slevin (Eds.), *Age matters: Realigning feminist thinking* (pp. 123–53). New York: Routledge.

Corbin, J. M., & Strauss, A. (1988). *Unending work and care: Managing chronic illness at home.* San Francisco. Jossey-Bass Publishers.

Cortese, A. J. P. (2008). *Provocateur: Images of women and minorities in advertising* (3rd ed). Lanham, MD: Rowman & Littlefield Publishers.

Crawford, R. (1980). Healthism and the medicalization of everyday life. *International Journal of Health Services, 10* (3), 365–88.

Crossley, N. (1995). Merleau-Ponty, the elusive body and carnal sociology. *Body and Society, 1* (1), 43–63.

Cruikshank, M. (2003). *Learning to be old: Gender, culture and aging.* Lanham, MD: Rowman & Littlefield Publishers.

Cuddy, A. J. C., Norton, M. I., & Fiske, S. T. (2005). This old stereotype: The pervasiveness and persistence of the elderly stereotype. *Journal of Social Issues, 61* (2), 267–85.

Davis, K. (1995). *Reshaping the female body: The dilemma of cosmetic surgery.* New York: Routledge.

Davis, K. (1997). "My body is my art": Cosmetic surgery as feminist utopia? *European Journal of Women's Studies, 4* (1), 23–37.

Davis, K. (2003). *Dubious equalities and embodied differences: Cultural studies on cosmetic surgery.* New York: Rowman & Littlefield Publishers.

de Beauvoir, S. (1952). *The second sex.* (H. M. Parshley, Trans.). New York: Knopf. (Original work published 1949.)

de Luce, J. (2001). Silence at the newsstands. *Generations, 25* (3), 39–43.

Demos, V., & Jache, A. (1981). When you care enough: An analysis of attitudes toward aging in humorous birthday cards. *The Gerontologist, 21* (2), 209–15.

Dillaway, H. (2005a). Menopause is the "good old": Women's thoughts about reproductive aging. *Gender and Society, 19* (3), 398–417.

Dillaway, H. (2005b). (Un)changing menopausal bodies: How women think and act in the fact of reproductive transition and gendered beauty ideals. *Sex Roles, 53* (1/2), 1–17.

Dillaway, H. (2007). "Am I similar to my mother?" How women make sense of menopause using family background. *Women and Health, 46* (1), 79–97.

Dillon, K., & Jones, B. S. (1981). Attitudes toward aging portrayed by birthday cards. *International Journal of Aging and Human Development, 13* (1), 79–84.

Dionne, M., Davis, C., Fox, J., & Gurevich, M. (1995). Feminist ideology as a predictor of body dissatisfaction in women. *Sex Roles, 33* (3/4), 277–87.

Dumas, A., Laberge, S., & Straka, S. M. (2005). Older women's relations to bodily appearance: The embodiment of social and biological conditions of existence. *Ageing and Society, 25* (6), 883–902.

Duncan, C., & Loretto, W. (2004). Never the right age? Gender and age-based discrimination in employment. *Gender, Work and Organization, 11* (1), 95–115.

Dworkin, A. (1974). *Woman hating.* New York: E. P. Dutton.

Dworkin, S. H. (1989). Not in a man's image: Lesbians and the cultural oppression of body image. *Women and Therapy, 8* (1), 27–39.

Dye, L. (2009). Consuming constructions: A critique of Dove's campaign for real beauty. *Canadian Journal of Media Studies, 5* (1), 114–28.

Dykes, F. (2005). "Supply" and "demand": Breastfeeding as labour. *Social Science and Medicine, 60* (10), 2283–93.

Earle, S. (2003). "Bumps and boobs": Fatness and women's experiences of pregnancy. *Women's Studies International Forum, 26* (3), 245–52.

Faircloth, C. A., Boylstein, C., Rittman, M., Young, M. E., & Gubrium, J. (2004). Sudden illness and biographical flow in narratives of stroke recovery. *Sociology of Health and Illness, 26* (2), 242–61.

Fairhurst, E. (1998). "Growing old gracefully" as opposed to "mutton dressed as lamb": The social construction of recognizing older women. In S. Nettleton & J. Watson (Eds.), *The body in everyday life* (pp. 1–24). New York: Routledge.

Falkingham, J., & Rake, K. (1999). Partnership in pensions: Delivering a secure retirement for women. *Benefits,* September/October, 11–15.

Featherstone, M., & Turner, S. B. (1995). Body and society: An introduction. *Body and Society, 1* (1), 1–12.

Featherstone, M., & Wernick, A. (1995). *Images of aging: Cultural representations of later life.* New York: Routledge.

Feingold, A., & Mazzella, R. (1998). Gender differences in body image are increasing. *Psychological Science, 9* (3), 190–95.

Findlay, D. A., & Miller, L. J. (2002). Through medical eyes: The medicalization of women's bodies and women's lives. In B. S. Bolaria & H. D. Dickinson (Eds.), *Health, illness, and health care in Canada* (3rd ed.) (pp. 185–210). Scarborough, ON: Nelson Thomson Learning.

Fishman, J. R., Binstock, B. H., & Lambrix, M. A. (2008). Anti-aging science: The emergence, maintenance, and enhancement of a discipline. *Journal of Aging Studies, 22* (3), 295–303.

Fishman, J. R., Settersten, Jr., R. A., & Flatt, M. A. (2010). In the vanguard of biomedicine? The curious and contradictory case of anti-ageing medicine. *Sociology of Health and Illness, 32* (2), 197–210.

Forbes.com. (2008). The world's biggest companies. Last retrieved from www.forbes.com/2008/04/02/worlds-largest-companies-biz-2000global08-cx_sd_0402global_land.html on November 1, 2008.

Forbes, G. B., & Frederick, D. A. (2008). The UCLA Body Project II: Breast and body dissatisfaction among African, Asian, European, and Hispanic American college women. *Sex Roles, 58* (7–8), 449–57.

Foucault, M. (1979). *Discipline and punish: The birth of a prison*. New York: Vintage Books.

Franzoi, S. L. (1995). The body-as-object versus the body-as-process: Gender differences and gender considerations. *Sex Roles*, 33 (5/6), 417–37.

Franzoi, S. L., & Koehler, V. (1998). Age and gender differences in body attitudes: A comparison of young and elderly adults. *International Journal of Aging and Human Development*, 47 (1), 1–10.

Fraser, S. (2003). *Cosmetic surgery, gender and culture*. New York: Palgrave MacMillan.

Freund, P. E. S., McGuire, M. B., & Podhurst, L. S. (2003). *Health, illness, and the social body: A critical sociology* (4th ed.). Upper Saddle River, NJ: Prentice-Hall.

Frith, K. T., Shaw, P., & Cheng, H. (2005). The construction of beauty: A cross-cultural analysis of women's magazine advertising. *The Journal of Communication*, 55 (1), 56–70.

Frost, L. (2001). *Young women and the body: A feminist sociology*. New York: Palgrave Macmillan.

Furman, F. K. (1997). *Facing the mirror: Older women and beauty shop culture*. New York: Routledge.

Gerike, A. E. (1990). On grey hair and oppressed brains. *Women, Aging, and Ageism*, 2 (2), 35–46.

Gibson, H. B. (1993). Emotional and sexual adjustment in later life. In S. Arber & M. Evandrou (Eds.), *Ageing, independency and the life course* (pp. 104–18). London: Jessica Kingsley Publishers.

Gibson, M. (2006). Bodies without histories: Cosmetic surgery and the undoing of time. *Australian Feminist Studies*, 21 (49), 51–63.

Gimlin, D. L. (1996). Pamela's place: Power and negotiation in the hair salon. *Gender and Society*, 10 (5), 505–26.

Gimlin, D. L. (2000). Cosmetic surgery: Beauty as commodity. *Qualitative Sociology*, 23 (1), 77–98.

Gimlin, D. L. (2002). *Body work: Beauty and self-image in American culture*. Los Angeles: University of California Press.

Ginn, J., & Arber, S. (1993). Pension penalties: The gendered division of occupational warfare. *Work, Employment and Society*, 7 (1), 47–70.

Ginn, J., & Arber, S. (1995). "Only connect": Gender relations and ageing. In S. Arber and J. Ginn (Eds.), *Connecting gender and ageing: A sociological approach* (pp. 1–14). Buckingham, UK: Open University Press.

Ginn, J., & Arber, S. (1996). Gender, age and attitudes to retirement in mid-life. *Ageing and Society*, 16 (1), 27–55.

Goffman, E. (1963). *Stigma: Notes on the management of spoiled identity*. Englewood Cliffs, NJ: Prentice-Hall.

Gott, M., & Hinchliff, S. (2003). How important is sex in later life? The views of older people. *Social Science and Medicine*, 56 (8), 1617–28.

Gott, M., Hinchliff, S., & Galena, E. (2004). General practitioner attitudes to discussing sexual health issues with older people. *Social Science and Medicine, 58* (1), 2093–2103.

Greene, M. G., Adelman, R. D., & Rizzo, C. (1996). Problems in communication between physicians and older patients. *Journal of Geriatric Psychiatry, 29* (1), 13–32.

Grenier, A., & Hanley, J. (2007). Older women and "frailty": Aged, gendered and embodied resistance. *Current Sociology, 55* (2), 211–28.

Grogan, S. (2008). *Body image: Understanding body dissatisfaction in men, women, and children* (2nd ed.). New York: Routledge.

Gubrium, J. F., & Holstein, J. A. (2003). The everyday visibility of the aging body. In C. A. Faircloth (Ed.), *Aging bodies: Images and everyday experience* (pp. 205–27). New York: AltaMira.

Gullette, M. M. (2004). *Aged by culture*. Chicago: The University of Chicago Press.

Hallinan, C. J., & Schuler, P. B. (1993). Body-shape perceptions of elderly women exercisers and nonexercisers. *Perceptual and Motor Skills, 77* (2), 451–56.

Halliwell, E., & Dittmar, H. (2003). A qualitative investigation of women's and men's body image and their attitudes toward aging. *Sex Roles, 49* (11/12), 675–84.

Harding, J. (1997). Bodies at risk: Sex, surveillance, and hormone replacement therapy. In A. R. Petersen & R. Bunton (Eds.), *Foucault, health and medicine* (pp. 134–50). New York: Routledge.

Harris, M. B., Walters, L. C., & Waschull, S. (1991). Gender and ethnic differences in obesity-related behaviors and attitudes in a college sample. *Journal of Applied Social Psychology, 21* (19), 1545–66.

Harwood, J., & Roy, A. (1999). The portrayal of older adults in Indian and U.S. magazine advertisements. *The Howard Journal of Communications, 10* (4), 269–80.

Healey, S. (1993). Confronting ageism: A MUST for mental health. In N. D. Davis, E. Cole, & E. D. Rothblum (Eds.), *Faces of women and aging* (pp. 41–54). New York: Harrington Park.

Healey, T., & Ross, K. (2002). Growing old invisibly: Older viewers talk television. *Media, Culture, and Society, 24* (1), 105–20.

Henderson-King, D., & Henderson-King, E. (2005). Acceptance of cosmetic surgery: Scale development and validation. *Body Image, 2* (2), 137–49.

Henderson-King, E., & Henderson-King, D. H. (1997). Media effects on women's body esteem: Social and individual difference factors. *Journal of Applied Social Psychology, 27* (5), 399–417.

Hennessy, C. H. (1989). Culture in the use, care, and control of the aging body. *Journal of Aging Studies, 3* (1), 39–54.

Herzog, D. B., Newman, K. L., Yeh, C. J., & Warshaw, M. (1992). Body image satisfaction in homosexual and heterosexual women. *International Journal of Eating Disorders, 11* (4), 391–96.

Hesse-Biber, S. N. (1996). *Am I thin enough yet? The cult of thinness and the commercialization of identity.* New York: Oxford University Press.

Hesse-Biber, S. N., Howling, S. A., Leavy, P., & Lovejoy, M. (2004). Racial identity and the development of body image issues among African American adolescent girls. *The Qualitative Report, 9* (1), 49–79.

Hinchliff, S., & Gott, M. (2008). Challenging social myths and stereotypes of women and aging: Heterosexual women talk about sex. *Journal of Women and Aging, 20* (1/2), 65–81.

Hochschild, A. (1973). *The unexpected community.* Englewood Cliffs, NJ: Prentice-Hall.

Holstein, M. B. (2001). A feminist perspective on anti-aging medicine. *Generations, 25* (4), 38–43.

Holstein, M. B. (2006). On being an aging woman. In T. M. Calasanti & K. F. Slevin (Eds.), *Age matters: Realigning feminist thinking* (pp. 313–34). New York: Routledge.

Holsti, O. R. (1969). *Content analysis for the social sciences and humanities.* Reading, MA: Addison-Wesley Publishing Company.

Hurd, L. (1999). "We're not old!": Older women's negotiation of aging and oldness. *Journal of Aging Studies, 13* (4), 419–39.

Hurd, L. (2000). Older women's body image and embodied experience: An exploration. *Journal of Women and Aging, 12* (3/4), 77–97.

Hurd Clarke, L. (2001). Older women's bodies and the self: The construction of identity in later life. *Canadian Review of Sociology and Anthropology, 38* (4), 441–64.

Hurd Clarke, L. (2002a). Beauty in later life: Older women's perceptions of physical attractiveness. *Canadian Journal on Aging, 21* (3), 429–42.

Hurd Clarke, L. (2002b). Older women's perceptions of ideal body weights: The tensions between health and appearance motivations for weight loss. *Ageing and Society, 22* (6), 751–73.

Hurd Clarke, L. (2003). Overcoming ambivalence: The challenges of exploring socially charged issues. *Qualitative Health Research, 13* (5), 718–35.

Hurd Clarke, L. (2006). Older women and sexuality: Experiences in marital relationships across the life course. *Canadian Journal on Aging, 25* (2), 129–40.

Hurd Clarke, L., & Bundon, A. (2009). From "the thing to do" to "defying the ravages of age": Older women reflect on the use of lipstick. *Journal of Women and Aging, 21* (3), 198–212.

Hurd Clarke, L., & Griffin, M. (2007a). The body natural and the body unnatural: Beauty work and aging. *Journal of Aging Studies, 21* (3), 187–201.

Hurd Clarke, L., & Griffin, M. (2007b). Becoming and being gendered through the body: Older women, mothers and body image. *Ageing and Society, 27* (5), 701–18.

Hurd Clarke, L., & Griffin, M. (2008a). Body image and aging: Older women and the embodiment of trauma. *Women's Studies International Forum, 31* (3), 200–208.

Hurd Clarke, L., & Griffin, M. (2008b). Visible and invisible ageing: Beauty work as a response to ageism. *Ageing and Society, 28* (5), 653–74.

Hurd Clarke, L., Griffin, M., & Maliha, K. (2009). Bat wings, bunions, and turkey wattles: Body transgressions and older women's strategic clothing choices. *Ageing and Society, 29* (5), 709–26.

Hurd Clarke, L., & Korotchenko, A. (2009). Older women and suntanning: The negotiation of health and appearance risks. *Sociology of Health and Illness, 31* (5), 748–61.

Hurd Clarke, L., & Korotchenko, A. (2010). Shades of grey: To dye or not to dye one's hair in later life. *Ageing and Society, 30* (in press).

Hurd Clarke, L., Repta, R., & Griffin, M. (2007). Non-surgical cosmetic procedures: Older women's perceptions and experiences. *Journal of Women and Aging, 19* (3/4), 69–87.

Itzin, C., & Phillipson, C. (1993). Age barriers at work: Maximising the potential of mature and older workers. Metropolitan Authorities Recruitment Agency, Solihull, West Midlands, UK.

Itzin, C., & Phillipson, C. (1995). Gendered ageism: A double jeopardy for women in organizations. In C. Itzen & J. Newman (Eds.), *Gender, culture and organizational change: Putting theory into practice* (pp. 81–90). London: Routledge.

Jeffreys, S. (2005). *Beauty and misogyny: Harmful cultural practices in the West.* New York: Routledge.

Johnston, J., & Taylor, J. (2008). Feminist consumerism and fat activists: A comparative study of grassroots activism and the Dove Real Beauty Campaign. *Signs: Journal of Women in Culture and Society, 33* (4), 941–66.

Johnston, L. (1996). Flexing femininity: Female body-builders refiguring the body. *Gender, Place, and Culture, 3* (3), 327–40.

Kane, R. L., & Kane, R. A. (2005). Ageism in healthcare and long-term care. *Generations, 29* (3), 49–54.

Katz, S. (2000). Busy bodies: Activity, aging, and the management of everyday life. *Journal of Aging Studies, 14* (2), 135–52.

Katz, S. (2001). Growing older without aging? Positive aging, anti-ageism, and anti-aging. *Generations, 25* (4), 27–32.

Kaufert, P. A. (1982). Myth and the menopause. *Sociology of Health and Illness, 4* (2), 141–66.

Kessler, E., Rakoczy, K., & Staudinger, U. M. (2004). The portrayal of older people in prime time television series: The match with gerontological evidence. *Ageing and Society, 24* (4), 531–52.

Kilbourne, J. (1994). Still killing us softly: Advertising and the obsession with thinness. In P. Fallon, M. A. Katzman, & S. C. Wooley (Eds.), *Feminist perspectives on eating disorders* (pp. 395–418). New York: The Guilford Press.

Kilbourne, J. (1999). *Deadly persuasion: Why women and girls must fight the addictive power of advertising.* New York: Free Press.

Kinnunen, T. (2010). "A second youth": Pursuing happiness and respectability through cosmetic surgery in Finland. *Sociology of Health and Illness, 32* (2), 258–71.

Kite, M. E., & Wagner, L. S. (2002). Attitudes towards older adults. In T. D. Nelson (Ed.), *Ageism: Stereotyping and prejudice against older persons* (pp. 129–61). Cambridge: MIT Press.

Kontos, P. C. (2004). Ethnographic reflections on selfhood, embodiment and Alzheimer's disease. *Ageing and Society, 24* (6), 829–49.

Kontula, O., & Haavio-Mannila, E. (2009). The impact of aging on human sexual activity and sexual desire. *Journal of Sex Research, 46* (1), 46–56.

Koppelman, C. (1996). The politics of hair. *Frontiers: A Journal of Women's Studies, 17* (2), 87–88.

Kotarba, J., & Held, M. (2006). Professional female football players: Tackling like a girl? In D. Waskul and P. Vannini (Eds.), *Body/embodiment: Symbolic interaction and the sociology of the body* (pp. 153–64). Burlington, VT: Ashgate.

Kuczynski, A. (1998, April 12). Anti-aging potion or poison? *New York Times.* Last retrieved from www.nytimes.com/1998/04/12/style/anti-aging-potion-or-poison.html on April 19, 2010.

Kwan, S., & Trautner, M. N. (2009). Beauty work: Individual and institutional rewards, the reproduction of gender, and questions of agency. *Sociology Compass, 3* (1), 49–71.

Lamb, C. S., Jackson, L. A., Cassiday, P. B., & Priest, D. J. (1993). Body figure preferences of men and women: A comparison of two generations. *Sex Roles, 28* (5/6), 345–58.

Lash, S. (1991). Genealogy and the body: Foucault/Deleuze/Nietzsche. In M. Featherstone, M. Hepworth, & B. S. Turner (Eds.), *The body: Social process and cultural theory* (pp. 256–80). Newbury Park, CA: Sage.

Laws, G. (1995). Understanding ageism: Lessons from feminism and postmodernism. *The Gerontologist, 35* (1), 112–18.

Laz, C. (1998). Act your age. *Sociological Forum, 13* (1), 85–113.

Laz, C. (2003). Age embodied. *Journal of Aging Studies, 17* (4), 503–19.

Leavy, P. L. (2007). The feminist practice of content analysis. In S. N. Hesse-Biber and P. L. Leavy (Eds.), *Feminist research practice: A primer* (pp. 223–48). Thousand Oaks, CA: Sage.

Leder, D. (1984). Medicine and paradigms of embodiment. *The Journal of Medicine and Philosophy, 9*, 29–43.

Leder, D. (1990). *The absent body.* Chicago: University of Chicago Press.

Lee, C. (1998). *Women's health: Psychological and social perspectives.* Thousand Oaks, CA: Sage.

Lee, J. (1997). Never innocent: Breasted experience in women's bodily narratives of puberty. *Feminism and Psychology, 7* (4), 453–74.

Lee, J. (2009). Bodies at menarche: Stories of shame, concealment, and sexual maturation. *Sex Roles, 60* (9/10), 615–27.

Lee, J., & Sasser-Coen, J. (1996). Memories of menarche: Older women remember their first period. *Journal of Aging Studies, 10* (2), 83–101.

Leiss, W., Kline, S., Jhally, S., & Botterill, J. (2005). *Social communication in advertising: Consumption in the mediated marketplace* (3rd ed.). New York: Routledge.

Lende, D. H., & Lachiondo, A. (2009). Embodiment and breast cancer among African American women. *Qualitative Health Research, 19* (2), 216–28.

Lorber, J., & Moore, L. J. (2007). *Gendered bodies: Feminist perspectives.* Los Angeles, CA: Roxbury Publishing Company.

Lupton, D. (1999). Risk and the ontology of pregnant embodiment. In D. Lupton (Ed.), *Risk and sociocultural theory: New directions and perspectives* (pp. 59–85). Cambridge: Cambridge University Press.

Mackey, S. (2007). Women's experience of being well during peri-menopause: A phenomenological study. *Contemporary Nurse, 25* (1/2), 39–49.

Magazine Publishers of America (2009). Average circulation for top 100 ABC magazines 2005 [Data file]. Retrieved from www.magazine.org/CONSUMER_MARKETING/CIRC_TRENDS/16117.aspx on April 24, 2009.

Markson, E. W., & Taylor, C. A. (2000). The mirror has two faces. *Ageing and Society, 20* (2), 137–60.

Markula, P. (1995). Beyond the perfect body: Women's body image distortion in fitness magazine discourse. *Journal of Sport and Social Issues, 25* (2), 158–79.

Martin, E. (1987). *The woman in the body.* Boston: Beacon.

McCann, R., & Giles, H. (2002). Ageism in the workplace: A communication in perspective. In T. D. Nelson (Ed.), *Ageism: Stereotyping and prejudice against older persons* (pp. 163–99). Cambridge: MIT Press.

McCormack, J. (2002). Acute hospitals and older people in Australia. *Ageing and Society, 22* (5), 637–46.

McLaren, L., & Kuh, D. (2004a). Body dissatisfaction in midlife women. *Journal of Women and Aging, 16* (1/2), 35–54.

McLaren, L., & Kuh, D. (2004b). Women's body dissatisfaction, social class, and social mobility. *Social Science and Medicine, 58* (9), 1575–84.

McMullin, J. A., & Berger, E. D. (2006). Gendered ageism/age(ed) sexism: The case of unemployed older workers. In T. M. Calasanti & K. F. Slevin (Eds.), *Age matters: Realigning feminist thinking* (pp. 201–23). New York: Routledge.

McMullin, J. A., & Marshall, V. W. (2001). Ageism, age relations, and garment industry work in Montreal. *The Gerontologist, 41* (1), 111–22.

McPherson, B. D. (1990). *Aging as a social process: An introduction to individual and population aging* (2nd ed.). Toronto: Butterworths.

Merleau-Ponty, M. (1962). *Phenomenology of perception* (C. Smith, Trans.). New York: Routledge and Kegan Paul. (Original work published 1945.)

Millsted, R., & Frith, H. (2003). Being large-breasted: Women negotiating embodiment. *Women's Studies International Forum, 26* (5), 455–65.

Minichiello, V., Browne, J. & Kendig, H. (2000). Perceptions and consequences of agcism. Views of older people. *Ageing and Society, 20* (3), 253–78.

Molloy, B. L., & Herzberger, S. D. (1998). Body image and self-esteem: A comparison of African-American and Caucasian women. *Sex Roles, 38* (7/8), 631–43.

Morris, M. E., & Symonds, A. (2004). "We've been trained to put up with it": Real women and menopause. *Critical Public Health, 14* (3), 311–23.

Muth, J. L., & Cash, T. F. (1997). Body-image attitudes: What difference does gender make? *Journal of Applied Social Psychology, 27* (16), 1438–52.

Myers, Jr., P. N., & Biocca, F. A. (1992). The elastic body image: The effect of television advertising and programming on body image distortions in young women. *Journal of Communications, 42* (3), 108–33.

Mykytyn, C. E. (2006). Anti-aging medicine: A patient/practitioner movement to redefine aging. *Social Science and Medicine, 62* (3), 643–653.

Mykytyn, C. E. (2008). Medicalizing the optimal: Anti-aging medicine and the quandary of intervention. *Journal of Aging Studies, 22* (3), 313–21.

Negrin, L. (2002). Cosmetic surgery and the eclipse of identity. *Body and Society, 8* (4), 21–42.

Nelson, T. D. (2005). Ageism: Prejudice against our feared future self. *Journal of Social Issues, 61* (2), 207–21.

Nettleton, S., & Watson, J. (1998). The body in everyday life: An introduction. In S. Nettleton, & J. Watson (Eds.), *The body in everyday life* (pp. 1–23). New York: Routledge.

Oberg, P., & Tornstam, L. (2001). Youthfulness and fitness—Identity ideals for all ages? *Journal of Aging and Identity, 6* (1), 15–29.

Ogden, J., & Thomas, D. (1999). The role of familial values in understanding the impact of social class on weight concern. *International Journal of Eating Disorders, 25* (3), 273–79.

Orbach, S. (2009). *Bodies.* New York: Macmillan.

Palmore, E. B. (1999). *Ageism: Negative and positive* (2nd ed.). New York: Springer.

Paquette, M. C., & Raine, K. (2004). Sociocultural context of women's body image. *Social Science and Medicine, 59* (5), 1047–58.

Perz, J., & Ussher, J. M. (2008). "The horror of this living decay": Women's negotiation and resistance of medical discourses around menopause and midlife. *Women's Studies International Forum, 31* (4), 293–99.

Phinney, A., & Chesla, C. A. (2003). The lived body in dementia. *Journal of Aging Studies, 17* (3), 283–99.

Pitman, G. E. (2000). The influence of race, ethnicity, class, and sexual politics on lesbians' body image. *Journal of Homosexuality, 40* (2), 49–64.

Pliner, P., Chaiken, S., & Flett, G. L. (1990). Gender differences in concern with body weight and physical appearance over the life span. *Personality and Social Psychology Bulletin, 16* (2), 263–73.

Pozner, J. L. (2005). Dove's "real beauty" backlash. *Bitch: Feminist Response to Pop Culture, 30.* Last retrieved from www.wimnonline.org/articles/dove backlash.html on April 22, 2010.

Quadagno, J. S. (1999). *Aging and the life course.* Boston: McGraw-Hill.

Rambo, C., Presley, S. R., & Mynatt, D. (2006). Claiming the bodies of exotic dancers: The problematic discourse of commodification. In D. Waskul & P. Vannini (Eds.), *Body/embodiment: Symbolic interaction and the sociology of the body* (pp. 213–28). Burlington, VT: Ashgate.

Ratan, D., Gandhi, D., & Palmer, R. (1998). Eating disorders in British Asians. *International Journal of Eating Disorders, 24* (1), 101–5.

Reboussin, B. A., Rejeski, W. J., Martin, K. A., Callahan, K., Dunn, A. L., King, A. C., & Sallis, J. F. (2000). Correlates of satisfaction with body function and body appearance in middle- and older-aged adults: The activity counseling trial. *Psychology and Health, 15* (2), 239–54.

Riessman, C. K. (1998). Women and medicalization: A new perspective. In R. Weitz (Ed.), *The politics of women's bodies: Sexuality, appearance and behavior* (pp. 46–63). New York: Oxford University Press.

Roberto, K. A. (1990). Adjusting to chronic disease: The osteoporotic woman. *Journal of Women and Aging, 2* (1), 33–47.

Rodin, J. (1992). Body mania. *Psychology Today, 25* (1), 56–60.

Rodin, J., Silberstein, L., & Striegel-Moore, R. (1985). Women and weight: A normative discontent. In T. B. Sonderegger (Ed.), *Nebraska symposium on motivation, 32, Psychology and gender* (pp. 267–307). Lincoln: University of Nebraska Press.

Rosenfeld, D., & Faircloth, C. (2004). Embodied fluidity and the commitment to movement: Constructing the moral self through arthritis narratives. *Symbolic Interaction, 27* (4), 507–29.

Sanders, C., Donovan, J., & Dieppe, P. (2002). The significance and consequences of having painful and disabled joints in older age: Co-existing accounts of normal and disrupted biographies. *Sociology of Health and Illness, 24* (2), 227–53.

Schmied, V., & Barclay, L. (1999). Connection and pleasure, disruption and distress: Women's experiences of breastfeeding. *Journal of Human Lactation, 15* (4), 325–34.

Schmied, V., & Lupton, D. (2001). Blurring the boundaries: Breastfeeding and maternal subjectivity. *Sociology of Health and Illness, 23* (2), 234–50.

Secunda, V. (1984). *By youth possessed.* New York: Bobbs-Merrill.

Seid, R. P. (1989). *Never too thin: Why women are at war with their bodies.* Toronto: Prentice-Hall.

Seid, R. P. (1994). Too "close to the bone": The historical context for women's obsession with slenderness. In P. Fallon, M. A. Katzman, & S. C. Wooley (Eds.), *Feminist perspectives on eating disorders* (pp. 3 16). New York: The Guilford Press.

Shilling, C. (2003). *The body and social theory* (2nd ed.). Thousand Oaks, CA: Sage.

Siegal, D. L. (1992). Women's reproductive changes: A marker, not a turning point. In L. Glasse & J. Hendricks (Eds.), *Gender and aging* (pp. 53–57). Amityville, NY: Baywood.

Siever, M. D. (1994). Sexual orientation and gender as factors in socioculturally acquired vulnerability to body dissatisfaction and eating disorders. *Journal of Consulting and Clinical Psychology, 62* (2), 252–60.

Slevin, K. F. (2006). The embodied experiences of old lesbians. In T. M. Calasanti and K. F. Slevin (Eds.), *Age matters: Realigning feminist thinking* (pp. 247–68). New York: Routledge.

Smith, D. E. (1987). *The everyday world as problematic: A feminist sociology.* Boston: Northeastern University Press.

Sontag, S. (1972). The double standard of aging. *Saturday Review of the Society,* 23 (September), 29–38.

Spitzer, B. L., Henderson, K. A., & Zivian, M. T. (1999). Gender differences in population versus media body sizes: A comparison over four decades. *Sex Roles, 40* (7/8), 545–65.

Statistics Canada. (2008). Low income cut-offs for 2007 and low income measures for 2006. Ottawa: Minister of Industry. Last retrieved from www .statcan.gc.ca/pub/75f0002m/75f0002m2008004-eng.pdf on April 30, 2009.

Stevens, C., & Tiggemann, M. (1998). Women's body figure preferences across the life span. *The Journal of Genetic Psychology, 159* (1), 94–102.

Strauss, E. (1963). *The primary world of senses.* Glencoe, NY: The Free Press of Glencoe.

Striegel-Moore, R. H., & Franko, D. I. (2002). Body image issues among girls and women. In T. F. Cash & T. Pruzinsky (Eds.), *Body image: A handbook of theory, research, and clinical practice* (pp. 183–91). New York: Guilford.

Striegel-Moore, R. H., Tucker, N., & Hsu, J. (1990). Body image dissatisfaction and disordered eating in lesbian college students. *International Journal of Eating Disorders, 9* (5), 493–500.

Sussman, N. M., Truong, N., & Lim, J. (2007). Who experiences "America the beautiful"? Ethnicity moderating the effect of acculturation on body image and risks for eating disorders among immigrant women. *International Journal of Intercultural Relations, 31* (1), 29–49.

Symonds, A., & Holland, C. (2008). The same hairdo: The production of the stereotyped image of the older woman. In R. Ward & B. Bytheway (Eds.), *Researching age and multiple discrimination* (pp. 26–44). London: Centre for Policy on Ageing.

Synnott, A. (1987). Shame and glory: A sociology of hair. *British Journal of Sociology, 38* (3), 381–413.

Taub, J. (2003). What should I wear? A qualitative look at the impact of feminism and women's communities on bisexual women's appearance. *Journal of Bisexuality, 3* (1), 11–22.

Taylor, P., & Walker, A. (1998). Employers and older workers: Attitudes and employment practices. *Ageing and Society, 18* (6), 641–58.

Thomas, V. G., & James, M. D. (1988). Body image, dieting tendencies, and sex role traits in urban black women. *Sex Roles, 18* (9/10), 523–29.

Thomas-MacLean, R. (2005). Beyond dichotomies of health and illness: Life after breast cancer. *Nursing Inquiry, 12* (3), 200–209.

Tiggemann, M., & Lynch, J. E. (2001). Body image across the life span in adult women: The role of self-objectification. *Developmental Psychology, 37* (2), 243–53.

Tunaley, J. R., Walsh, S., & Nicolson, P. (1999). "I'm not bad for my age": The meaning of body size and eating in the lives of older women. *Ageing and Society, 19* (6), 741–59.

Turner, B. S. (1984). *The body and society: Explorations in social theory.* New York: Basil Blackwell.

Twigg, J. (1997). Deconstructing the "social" bath: Help with bathing at home for older and disabled people. *Journal of Social Policy, 26* (2), 211–32.

Twigg, J. (2004). The body, gender, and age: Feminist insights in social gerontology. *Journal of Aging Studies, 18* (1), 59–73.

Tyler, M., & Hancock, P. (2001). Flight attendants and the management of gendered "organizational bodies." In K. Backett-Milburn and L. McKie (Eds.), *Constructing gendered bodies* (pp. 25–38). New York: Palgrave.

Vernon, J. A., Williams, J. A., Phillips, T., & Wilson, J. (1990). Media stereotyping: A comparison of the way elderly women and men are portrayed on prime-time television. *Journal of Women and Aging, 2* (4), 55–68.

Walker, H., Grant, D., Meadows, M., & Cook, I. (2007). Women's experiences and perceptions of age discrimination in employment: Implications for research and policy. *Social Policy and Society, 6* (1), 37–48.

Wardle, J., & Griffith, J. (2001). Socioeconomic status and weight control practices in British adults. *Journal of Epidemiology and Community Health, 55* (3), 185–90.

Weitz, R. (2001). Women and their hair: Seeking power through resistance and accommodation. *Gender & Society, 15* (5), 667–86.

Weitz, R. (2005). *Rapunzel's daughters: What women's hair tells us about women's lives.* New York: Farrar, Straus, and Giroux.

West, C., & Zimmerman, D. H. (1987). Doing gender. *Gender and Society, 1* (2), 125–51.

White, P., Young, K., & Gillett, J. (1995). Bodywork as a moral imperative: Some critical notes on health and fitness. *Leisure and Society, 18* (1), 159 82.

Wilkinc, S. (2001). Aging, chronic illness and self-concept: A study of women with osteoporosis. *Journal of Women and Aging, 13* (1), 73–92.

Williams, S. J. (1996). The vicissitudes of embodiment across the chronic illness trajectory. *Body and Society, 2* (2), 23–47.

Winterich, J. A. (2007). Aging, femininity, and the body: What appearance changes mean to women with age. *Gender Issues, 24* (3), 51–69.

Wolf, N. (1991). *The beauty myth.* Toronto: Vintage Books.

Woodward, K. (1999a). Introduction. In K. Woodward (Ed.), *Figuring age: Women, bodies, generations* (pp. ix–xxix). Bloomington: Indiana University Press.

Woodward, K. (Ed.). (1999b). *Figuring age: Women, bodies, generations.* Bloomington: Indiana University Press.

Yates, A., Edman, J., & Aruguete, M. (2004). Ethnic differences in BMI and body/self dissatisfaction among whites, Asian subgroups, Pacific Islanders, and African-Americans. *Journal of Adolescent Health, 34* (4), 300–307.

Young, I. M. (1984). Pregnant embodiment: Subjectivity and alienation. *Journal of Medicine and Philosophy, 9* (1), 45–62.

Young, I. M. (1990). *Throwing like a girl and other essays in feminist philosophy and social theory.* Bloomington: Indiana University Press.

# Index

advertising: 103; ageism in, 1, 8,
104–105, 113–14, 117; allusions
to cosmetic surgery, 106–108;
allusions to non-surgical cosmetic
procedures, 106–108; of anti-aging
products, 14–15, 73, 105–108, 126,
129; portrayals of aging in, 1,
14–15, 104–105, 107; older women's
perceptions of, 8, 105, 114–17, 119,
128

aesthetic medicine: experiences of
older women, 5, 7–9, 70, 82–96, 98;
surgeons' and physicians' roles, 7,
13–14, 74–75, 78. *See also* anti-aging
technologies

ageism: appearance and, 4, 23, 30–31,
43, 53, 57, 59–60, 65–67, 70, 74,
78–89, 96–97, 138; consumerism
and, 1, 30; cultural norms and,
1, 3, 5, 6, 8, 65; defined, 28–29;
devaluation of older women, 4,
23, 29–30, 43, 45, 53, 56, 59–60,
66–67, 80–81, 84, 96, 105, 109, 123;
discrimination, 2–4, 28–31, 56, 63,
66–67, 84, 86, 98, 116, 119, 120;
double standard of aging and,
30–31, 37, 42–43, 77–78, 132; as

embodied oppression, 3, 19, 29, 78;
gendered ageism, 3, 30, 57, 77–78,
96, 138–39; internalization of, 6, 8,
43, 45, 57, 63–64, 66–67, 79–80, 83,
86, 92, 116, 125, 130, 137; lack of
theorizing about, 2–3; mandatory
retirement, 3, 28–29; the media
and, 1, 2, 8, 73, 77, 104–109, 113–14,
116, 126, 128, 130; as othering, 29,
45; print advertisements and, 8,
104–109, 117, 126; resistance of,
5–6, 8, 59, 64, 66–67, 86–87; as self
oppression, 2–3, 65, 67, 97; sexism
and, 5–6, 30, 36, 42–43, 65, 77–78,
96, 114–15, 117, 120, 133, 135,
137–38; societal disregard of, 2–3;
stereotypes, 29–30, 80, 123; in the
workplace, 3, 28–30, 123

age relations: appearance and, 3, 6,
21, 30–31, 38; defined, 6, 17n1;
oppression, 3, 28–29

aging: aging bodies as unattractive,
2, 7, 30–31, 38–39, 43–44, 54, 57,
59–60, 65–67, 78–80, 98, 105, 109;
appearance, 5, 7, 30–31, 38, 43,
45, 54, 59–60, 62–64, 66–67, 70, 74,
79–80, 83, 86, 126–28, 135; beauty

# About the Author

**Laura Hurd Clarke** is an associate professor in sociology in the School of Human Kinetics at the University of British Columbia in Vancouver, Canada. She is also a Michael Smith Foundation for Health Research Career Investigator. Dr. Hurd Clarke's articles on aging, body image, and embodiment have been published in journals such as *Ageing and Society*, *Canadian Journal on Aging*, *Journal of Aging Studies*, *Qualitative Health Research*, and *Sociology of Health and Illness*. Her current research focuses on aging, illness, technology, and the body.